HE FIRST LOVED US

Twelve Lessons Revealing God's Love

ROBERT RIDINGS

WESTBOW
PRESS®
A DIVISION OF THOMAS NELSON
& ZONDERVAN

Scripture taken from the Holy Bible, NEW INTERNATIONAL VERSION®. Copyright © 1973, 1978, 1984 by Biblica, Inc. All rights reserved worldwide. Used by permission. NEW INTERNATIONAL VERSION® and NIV® are registered trademarks of Biblica, Inc. Use of either trademark for the offering of goods or services requires the prior written consent of Biblica US, Inc.

Scripture taken from the New King James Version. Copyright © 1979, 1980, 1982 by Thomas Nelson, Inc. Used by permission. All rights reserved.

WestBow Press books may be ordered through booksellers or by contacting:

WestBow Press
A Division of Thomas Nelson & Zondervan
1663 Liberty Drive
Bloomington, IN 47403
www.westbowpress.com
1 (866) 928-1240

Because of the dynamic nature of the Internet, any web addresses or links contained in this book may have changed since publication and may no longer be valid. The views expressed in this work are solely those of the author and do not necessarily reflect the views of the publisher, and the publisher hereby disclaims any responsibility for them.

Any people depicted in stock imagery provided by Thinkstock are models, and such images are being used for illustrative purposes only. Certain stock imagery © Thinkstock.

ISBN: 978-1-5127-3572-7 (sc)
ISBN: 978-1-5127-3571-0 (e)

Library of Congress Control Number: 2016904715

Print information available on the last page.

WestBow Press rev. date: 03/24/2016

Contents

Introduction

He First Loved Us consists of twelve lessons, each revealing God's love for us. Each lesson has questions to promote discussion. These lessons can be used as a twelve-week classroom study, or they can be used for your own private study.

God first loved us by paying for our sins himself, through his Son. This was God's plan to redeem us and to reveal his love to us. God desperately wants us to know that he loves us and that we can trust him. The Word states, "And without faith it is impossible to please God, because anyone who comes to him must believe that he exists and that he rewards those who earnestly seek him" (Hebrews 11:6). The Word also states, "And now these three remain: faith, hope and love. But the greatest of these is love" (1 Corinthians 13:13). Our faith and hope are born out of love. Jesus says to love the Lord and to love others are the greatest commandments. "'Love the Lord your God with all your heart and with all your soul and with all your strength and with all your mind'; and, 'Love your neighbor as yourself'" (Luke 10:27). It all starts by knowing in our heart that God loves us. Our hearts are forever being filled by God's love as we continually grow closer to him. Through his love, God is molding us to have the mind Christ, which is a process that continues all through our life until our last breath.

In this book, we will learn that we are created to have a mind of love and hope, and if we meditate on a God of love, it will help us both mentally and physically. The reality is that we are created to be filled with God's love because we are created to have the mind of Christ (1 Corinthians 2:16). Let this book bring you closer to the Lord and fill your heart with his love. A heart filled with God's love is a heart that is comforted with peace, joy, and security.

Lesson 1: God's Divine Plan

Introduction

You are part of a big story in God's divine plan. His plan reveals the purpose of your life and the perfect love God has for you. Understanding God's plan will help you better understand God and better understand his guidance in your life. Like anything in life, once we understand the plan, we are then able to complete the task.

Have you ever wondered why God created the heavens and the earth and why he created humanity? God is self-sufficient and needs nothing, yet he has a purpose for everything he says and does. He had a purpose for creating humanity, and he has a divine purpose for you and me. In this lesson, we will explore God's divine plan for humanity and the divine plan for your life.

God in Three Persons

Have you ever wondered why God reveals himself in three persons, Father, Son, and Spirit? All are God except they are separate, and God has always existed as the Trinity. God's divine plan is centered on humanity, and the Trinity is how he reveals himself to us. Christ came to Earth to show us how to live and to redeem us to God, and Christ asks the Father to send the Holy Spirit to live in the believer. The Trinity is God's perfect plan to reveal himself and his love to us.

God's Creation of the Heavens and the Earth

> In the beginning God created the heavens and the earth. (Genesis 1:1)

Genesis 1:1–25 tells us about God creating the heavens and the earth. He created the earth and all living things both on the land and in the sea. Note the beauty of God's creation: clouds, sunsets, green fields, oceans, trees, and the heavens as viewed on a clear night. The beauty of nature reveals the beauty of God's heart. God's creation provides a place for us to live our temporary, physical lives.

> Lift up your eyes and look to the heavens: Who created all these? He who brings out the starry host one by one and calls forth each of them by name. Because of his great power and mighty strength, not one of them is missing. (Isaiah 40:26)

If the heavens were created just for you and me, they are probably too big. However, I believe "The heavens declare the glory of God" (Psalm 19:1). The beauty of the universe shows the beauty of God, the enormous size of the universe shows his power, and the complexity of the universe shows his intelligence. The beauty of the earth and the heavens reveals the love that God has for us.

> For since the creation of the world God's invisible qualities—his eternal power and divine nature—have been clearly seen, being understood from what has been made, so that people are without excuse. (Romans 1:20)

Where do you see God's eternal power and divine nature?

_____

_____

_____   _____

What is your view of God when you notice the beauty of his creation?

_____

_____

_____

Satan Cast Out of Heaven

> And there was war broke in heaven. Michael and his angels fought against the dragon, and the dragon and his angels fought back. But he was not strong enough, and they lost their place in heaven. The great dragon was hurled down—that ancient serpent called the devil, or Satan, who leads the whole world astray. He was hurled to the earth, and his angels with him. (Revelation 12:7–9)

There is divine influence from God and sinful influence from Satan. God's influence is love, truth, and life to the fullest. Satan is the Father of Lies who came to kill, steal, and destroy; his goal is to lead the whole world astray, away from God.

What is the reason God cast Satan and his angels to the earth? Could he have destroyed Satan and his angels? God placed both good and evil in this world, the presence of both God and his angels and Satan and his angels. We have a choice to follow God or not to follow God. We show our love by trusting God and overcoming and enduring in this world. Is your choice to love God, trusting he will carry you through this life and into your heavenly home?

Explain why God cast Satan and his angels down to the earth.

_____

_____

_____

How do we think God wants us to show our love?

_____

_____

_____

Creation of Humanity

> Then the LORD God formed a man from the dust of the ground and breathed into his nostrils the breath of life, and the man became a living being. Now the LORD God had planted a garden in the east, in Eden; and there he put the man he had formed. (Genesis 2:7–8)

God created man (Truth Series by Focus on the Family),[1] from the dust of the ground and placed him in the garden of Eden. This garden was perfect, where Adam could live a perfect life in the presence of God. Adam had no companion that was suited for him and was alone, so God created a helper, a companion for Adam. He created woman.

> The LORD God said, "It is not good for the man to be alone; I will make him a helper suitable for him." (Genesis 2:18)

> So the LORD God caused the man to fall into a deep sleep; and while he was sleeping, he took one of the man's ribs and then closed up the place with flesh. Then the LORD God made a woman from the rib he had taken out of the man, and he brought her to the man. The man said, "This is now bone of my bones and flesh of my flesh; she shall be called 'woman,' for she was taken out of man." (Genesis 2:21–23)

> So God created mankind in his own image, in the image of God he created them; male and female he created them. (Genesis 1:27)

God's plan for us includes relationships, first with him and then with our family. This is God's design for our most meaningful relationships.

What does it mean to you that you are created in the image of God?

_____

_____

_____

Why are we to have our closest relationship with God?

_____

_____

_____

The Fall of Humanity

In Genesis 1:26–30 we read that God created everything for man to rule over, look after, and care for. The garden of Eden was a paradise until Adam and Eve chose to sin and the world was changed. God said in Genesis 3:17, "Cursed is the ground because of you," and Romans 8:22 says, "We know that the whole creation has been groaning as in the pains of childbirth right up to the present time."

In Genesis 3:1–6 we read that Adam and Eve sinned against God. They were told not to eat of the fruit from the Tree of Knowledge of Good and Evil located in the center of the garden. Satan tempted Eve, and both Adam and Eve ate of the fruit.

> But the LORD God called to the man, "Where are you?" He answered, "I heard you in the garden, and I was afraid because I was naked; so I hid." (Genesis 3:9–10)

The sinful and fearful nature is now inherited by all humanity. The Bible teaches that God is morally perfect and holy and hates sin. If God could live in the presence of sin, he would not be God, and if sin were allowed in heaven, it would not be heaven.

> But your iniquities have separated you from your God; your sins have hidden his face from you, so that he will not hear. (Isaiah 59:2)

Explain how Satan twisted the truth of God's words when he spoke to Eve.

_____

_____

_____

How do you think Adam and Eve felt after disobeying God?

_____

_____

_____

Redeeming Humanity

Adam's sin separated humanity from God, but God's divine plan reveals how he has redeemed us, so once again we can have a relationship with God.

> But God demonstrates his own love for us in this: While we were still sinners, Christ died for us. (Romans 5:8)

God provided a way to guide us through this sinful world: "the Lamb was slain from the creation of the world" (Revelation 13:8). He didn't abandon us. He took our sins on himself through Christ and fills us with the Holy Spirit so we can conquer the evils of this world when we repent and put our faith in Christ.

> For all have sinned and fall short of the glory of God. (Romans 3:23)

> Whoever does not love does not know God, because God is love. (1 John 4:8)

God created us in his image because he is love. We were created to love God and live with him for eternity, just as Adam was with God before sin. God's plan for our lives is to love us and bless us through Christ and bring us home with him forever. During our physical lives, we have a choice to make—to live for Christ or to live for Satan. There is no other choice. If we do not receive God's love and live for Christ, by default we are living for Satan. All who live for Christ will reap eternal glory, thereby fulfilling God's divine plan.

> For God so loved the world that he gave his one and only Son, that whoever believes in him shall not perish but have eternal life. (John 3:16)

Christ came to earth, born of a virgin, and lived a humble life as a servant and died for our sins on the cross. He reveals the heart of God and shows us how to live—humble and secure in Christ with a heart of love. Christ told his apostles, "They are not of the world" (John 17:16), and when we believe and accept Christ as our Savior, we are filled with the Spirit and are no longer of this world. Living in the Spirit, we are spiritually in the kingdom of God, which is within us (Luke 17:21). And like Christ, we live humble lives, serving and ministering to humanity. We are ambassadors of Christ (2 Corinthians 5:20) living in a foreign land; our home is in heaven with Christ.

What does it mean when Christ said, "They are not of this world"?

_____

_____

_____

Explain why 1 John 4:8 is true. "Whoever does not love does not know God, because God is love."

_____

_____

_____

God's Plan for You

> "For I know the plans I have for you," declares the LORD, "plans to prosper you
> and not to harm you, plans to give you hope and a future." (Jeremiah 29:11)

God's divine plan includes you and me. He has a plan for your life, and whatever you do, wherever you go, you can carry out God's plan by living life in a godly manner, guided by the Holy Spirit. We are to show Christ to everyone by our attitude and actions. You may never know the divine impact you can have on someone.

> Whatever you do, work at it with all your heart, as working for the Lord, not
> for human masters, since you know that you will receive an inheritance from
> the Lord as a reward. It is the Lord Christ you are serving. (Colossians 3:23–24)

If we follow this verse, it will help us to be more successful in everything we do, if we give God the glory for our successes. This is living for Christ, which molds us to be more like him, leading us to our eternal destiny.

God has a plan for your life and specifically created you for this plan. When you live following God's plan, you can live life to the fullest because his plan reveals the life you were created to live. Living God's plan will give you security because nothing in all creation can change God's plan for your life.

What interests do you have that God could use for your ministry?

_____

_____

_____

How can living the plan God has for you give you security?

_____

_____

_____

Summary

God's divine plan for you is to live for eternity with him in your heavenly home. He created the world for us to live temporarily in the physical life, where sin exists through Satan and love exists through God. We have free will because without free will, how can love exist since love is a choice? God saved us from our sins through his Son who paid the debt for our sins when he took the wrath of God on the cross, thereby redeeming us to God. When we accept Christ as our Savior, we are filled with the Holy Spirit. He is our deposit on eternal life and leads us through this life. God's greatest desire is for you to know his love and how much he wants to bless you and bring you home to live with him forever.

Lesson 2: Created in the Image of God

Introduction

> So God created man in his own image, in the image of God he created him;
> male and female he created them. (Genesis 1:27)

After reading the Genesis account of God creating man in his image, I began to wonder what it really meant to be created in God's image. I believe that if we understand how we are the image of God, we can more fully receive God's love, better understand his divine plan for us, and learn how to grow spiritually. Knowing how we are designed can help us live a fulfilling life if we live according to God's directions. We know that God has a divine plan for us (Jeremiah 29:11), and we will not truly know who we were created to be until we are free in Christ. I surrendered to Christ when I was fifty-nine years old and have come to realize that if I had not given my life to Christ, I never would have known the person God created me to be.

Below describes five ways we are created in the image of God.

1. Spiritual (Soul and Spirit)

> May God himself, the God of peace, sanctify you through and through. May
> your whole spirit, soul and body be kept blameless at the coming of our Lord
> Jesus Christ. (1 Thessalonians 5:23)

We are created with body, soul, and spirit. Our body is our flesh; the soul is our mind, emotions, and personality; and our spirit is our godly nature. The body is temporal, but the soul and spirit are eternal. The body comes from the earth and returns to the earth while the soul and spirit live for eternity. Our soul and spirit will live eternally with a spiritual body.

> So will it be with the resurrection of the dead. The body that is sown is
> perishable, it is raised imperishable; it is sown in dishonor, it is raised in glory;
> it is sown in weakness, it is raised in power; it is sown a natural body, it is
> raised a spiritual body. (1 Corinthians 15:42–44)

God has given us free will, and we have the choice to follow Christ or to follow Satan. Those are the only two options. God has given us a mind and a spirit, so with reason and conscience, we can make godly judgments. He has given us emotions so we can better understand him as he reveals his feelings in Scripture.

Why do you think God created humanity?

_____

_____

_____

Why do you think God created mankind with free will?

_____

_____

_____

2 Eternity in Our Heart

> He has made everything beautiful in its time. He has also set eternity in the human heart; yet no one can fathom what God has done from beginning to end. (Ecclesiastes 3:11)

Many Christians live each day with little or no thought of their eternal life. They tend to live with their hope in Christ only for this life. However, when they are old and on their deathbed they realize this life is short and then face stepping into eternity.

> If only for this life we have hope in Christ, we are of all people most to be pitied. (1 Corinthians 15:19)

Brian Thomas, M.S., in his article, *"Evidence of Eternity in Our Hearts,"* states:

> Now, a new research tactic reveals that belief in an eternal life apart from our bodies is hardwired into each of us, inadvertently confirming the Bible's message. Boston University conducted two studies on 283 children from Ecuador. The children were from two sources, some living in the jungle and some with religious training from the city. Surprisingly, both groups of students maintained that a core aspect in each person lives even without the body. (Our soul). Essentially, then, our tendency to believe in an immortal soul does not explicitly arise from religion—it's just a part of us. If God clearly says He put eternity in our hearts, it's no wonder that sociologists find it there. It appears that scientists are just now confirming what Scripture has said all along about our knowledge of eternity.[2]

We are truly created with eternity in our hearts, and it can be seen by the way we desire to live. We have a God-given desire to live a life of peace and joy, without troubles or boredom, always comfortable and content. This is what we all seek because this is the way God intended for us to live. This was the life Adam and Eve had before they sinned, and it will be our life in eternity with the Lord. There, we will live with perfect peace and joy, trouble free, never bored, perfectly comfortable, and perfectly content.

> However, as it is written: "What no eye has seen, what no ear has heard, and what no human mind has conceived" the things God has prepared for those who love him. (1 Corinthians 2:9)

Our eternal soul is seeking eternal peace and joy, which can only come from the eternal God. We cannot find this eternal peace and joy from the world because everything in the world is temporary. The Lord provides through the indwelling Holy Spirit what the world cannot provide. God is the only one who can satisfy our empty, searching soul.

Why did God put eternity in the heart of mankind?

_____

_____

_____

Explain how our eternal soul is fulfilled only by the eternal God.

_____

_____

_____

3 Relationships

We are created to have a relationship with God and to worship him with our lives. Dr. Tim Clinton and Dr. Joshua Straub in their book *God Attachment* states, "Empirical evidence is now showing that we are born with a desire for a relationship with a 'Transcendent Other' and that longing begins to reveal itself in children as young as three years of age."[3]

Dr. Jennings in *Is It Really This Simple* wrote,

> God tells us to worship Me because we actually adapt ourselves to the things we admire and devote ourselves to the things we idealize. Psychiatry calls it modeling, and in the Bible it is the law of worship: by beholding, we become changed. Our character actually becomes transformed to reflect that which we revere.[4]

And Clinton and Straub wrote, "*All* scientific research now shows that from the time a baby is born, a baby's brain is biologically already formed to connect in relationships."[5] They went on to say, "We are hardwired as human beings—truly created and programmed to long for deep, lasting, and satisfying relationships."[6]

> The Lord God said, "It is not good for the man to be alone. I will make a helper suitable for him." (Genesis 2:18)

> Just as a body, though one, has many parts, but all its many parts form one body, so it is with Christ. (1 Corinthians 12:12)

The "helper" was Adams's wife, and the "many parts" of the body are the church, whose head is Christ. We are created to have relationships, first with God through Christ and then with our spouse (if married), our family, and God's family, the church. We can have a closer relationship with the Lord because the Father and the Son make their home with us through the Holy Spirit (John 14:23). When you love God more than anything or anyone, your heart is open to receive all of God's love, and then you can reflect more love to others. A close divine relationship with the Lord gives us the security to reflect his love. We can open our hearts to truly love because we are sustained by God's perfect love.

> Anyone who loves their father or mother more than me is not worthy of me; anyone who loves their son or daughter more than me is not worthy of me. (Matthew 10:37)

Life is about relationships. Our worldly and spiritual success in this life depends on our relationship with God and with others in relationship with family, coworkers, church family, friends, and strangers. We are created to have meaningful relationships, and God's Word is all about relationships.

Explain why God wants us to love him more than anyone or anything in this life.

_____

_____

_____

How can close relationships help us through the difficulties of life?

_____

_____

_____

4 Renewing the Mind

> Do not conform to the pattern of this world, but be transformed by the renewing
> of your mind. (Romans 12:2)

God gave you the extraordinary ability to renew your mind. The ability to change the neural wiring in our brain is called neuroplasticity. This means that whatever we think about the most gets wired in our brain the most. The more we think about something, the more real estate it takes in our brain, and conversely, the less we think about something, the less real estate in takes in our brain.

> But we have the mind of Christ. (1 Corinthians 2:16)

It is a true blessing that our mind can be renewed, allowing godly thoughts to replace sinful, harmful thoughts. This means the longer you worship the Lord, read the Word, pray, and fellowship, the more your mind rewires to be like Christ. You are able to essentially be your own brain surgeon, removing toxic thoughts and exchanging them with godly thoughts by controlling the way you think.

In his book *The God-Shaped Brain*, Dr. Timothy Jennings says, "Just as the Bible teaches, to give is to live. This is how God designed life to function."[7] God is continually renewing our mind to be like the mind of Christ as he molds us, using all things that happen in our life.

> And we know that in all things God works for the good of those who love him,
> who have been called according to his purpose. (Romans 8:28)

Knowing that God uses everything to mold us to the mind of Christ helps us to understand his direction for us. God's goal is to renew our minds to be like the mind of Christ, enabling us to overcome the world (1 John 5:4). Knowing that God wants to make us more Christlike and that our brain renews by rewiring helps us to pray for spiritual growth, knowing it is the will of God. For example, if you want peace, strength, wisdom, or to overcome a sinful thought, pray for it. If you are angry or fearful, give it to God and pray for peace and comfort. Ask God to help you to renew your mind and to control your thinking.

Describe what it would be like to have the mind of Christ.

_____

_____

_____

What does it mean to "overcome the world"?

_____

_____

_____

5 Created for Love and Hope

First John 4:8 states, "God is love." Christ has a heart of love and compassion, which we can see from his sacrifice on the cross. He also showed love and compassion during his ministry by healing people, casting out demons, forgiving sins, and speaking words of truth. God is continually molding us through the Holy Spirit to have the mind of Christ and reflect his heart of love and hope. "The law of love is an expression of God's character and the template in which life is built," says Dr. Jennings.[8] It is God's desire for us to live with a heart of love filled with hope and peace, which he gives us through the Holy Spirit. God does not want us to live in negative emotions, such as fear, anxiety, anger, resentment, and impatience.

> Do not be anxious about anything, but in every situation, by prayer and petition, with thanksgiving, present your requests to God. And the peace of God, which transcends all understanding, will guard your hearts and your minds in Christ Jesus. (Philippians 4:6–7)

God created us to live this life trusting him and feeling secure in Christ with peace and joy that comes from him. Does a mind filled with fear, anxiety, anger, resentment, or unforgiveness represent the image of God? If Jesus did not live with these negative emotions, we should not live with these negative emotions. As God molds us from the old nature to the new nature, we overcome these negative emotions and replace them with love and hope.

Dr. Jennings states, "When we stop loving and giving, we close the heart and mind and isolate ourselves from God's limitless love. It is only by receiving his abundant love and allowing that love to flow through us to others that we grow."[9]

A heart to love and hope is a heart that is comforted, peaceful, content, and relaxed. Perfect love also casts out fear (1 John 4:18), which is a blessing because fear and anxiety is one of Satan's favorite weapons. In a later lesson, we will see that a heart of love is good for our mental and physical health.

How can a mind of love and hope give us peace and comfort?

_____

_____

_____

How can do we grow in God's love?

_____

_____

_____

Summary

God created us for a specific purpose: to have a relationship with him, to have the mind of Christ, and to live for eternity with him. In achieving his purpose, he created us as spiritual beings to worship him, have a renewable brain, a need for relationships, a heart for eternity, and a heart of love and hope. We are uniquely created by God to live with him forever in heaven, and this is the ultimate life for mankind. We are also uniquely created for our purpose here on earth. He created each of us with specific talents for our ministry in this life. When we follow Christ and he leads us into the ministry he has for us, we find we are living life to the fullest.

If we know how something is designed, we can operate it properly. If we know how we are designed, we know how we operate properly and what is most fulfilling to us. The Word of God becomes our operating manual that tells us how to live life to the fullest, how to handle situations in this life, and how to overcome trials and tribulations. God's Word gives us a divine purpose in life, a divine eternal destination, and the direction to our eternal destination.

God loves us infinitely, and we live by his grace and his favor. God created you and fills you with his Spirit, the Holy Spirit, because he wants a close, loving relationship with you to lead you through a fulfilling life with love, peace, and joy. And at your last breath, he will take you home to be with him forever to live in your heavenly home that is waiting for you.

Lesson 3: God's Forgiveness

Introduction

In this lesson, we will look at the forgiving relationship God had with the Israelite nation, David, and Saul. As you read about God's forgiving heart, you will have a better understanding of God and the relationship you can have with him. The goal is to truly see and grasp the depths of God's love as seen ultimately in his forgiveness through Christ. We will read Scriptures about Christ becoming the Lamb of God, taking all the sins of the world to the cross and redeeming humanity to God. We can live each day in thankfulness for God's grace, accept his forgiveness, and forgive others and ourselves.

A Repentant Heart

> But if a wicked person turns away from all the sins they have committed and keeps all my decrees and does what is just and right, that person will surely live; they will not die. None of the offenses they have committed will be remembered against them. Because of the righteous things they have done, they will live. (Ezekiel 18:21–22)

The phrase "turns from all the sins" means to have a repentant heart, a heart that persists in overcoming sin. If we have godly sorrow for our sins and ask for forgiveness with a repentant heart, our transgressions are remembered no longer; this is the perfect forgiveness from God.

> The LORD our God is merciful and forgiving, even though we have rebelled against him. (Daniel 9:9)

Israel complained and sinned by worshipping idols and suffered the consequences for their disobedience to God. They rebelled against God and refused to listen to the prophets of God.

> They refused to listen and failed to remember the miracles you performed among them. They became stiff-necked and in their rebellion appointed a leader in order to return to their slavery. But you are a forgiving God, gracious

15

and compassionate, slow to anger and abounding in love. Therefore you did not desert them. (Nehemiah 9:17)

The Lord continually forgave the Israelites when they revealed a repentant heart and asked for forgiveness.

"Return, faithless Israel," declares the LORD; "I will not look upon you in anger. For I am gracious," declares the LORD; "I will not be angry forever. Only acknowledge your iniquity, That you have transgressed against the LORD your God." (Jeremiah 3:12-13)

God is eager to forgive whenever we have a repentant heart that seeks to turn away from our sinful behavior. He desires to fill us with his love and guide us through life, knowing his will for us is always the most fulfilling.

Describe a repentant heart.

_____

_____

_____

Identify anything that has a higher priority in your life than God.

_____

_____

_____

Godly Sorrow and Worldly Sorrow

God called David a man after his own heart, and the story of David's sin with Bathsheba is a powerful story of God's heart of love, mercy, and forgiveness.

One evening David got up from his bed and walked around on the roof of the palace. From the roof he saw a woman bathing. The woman was very beautiful, and David sent someone to find out about her. The man said, "She is Bathsheba, the daughter of Eliam and the wife of Uriah the Hittite." Then David sent messengers to get her. She came to him, and he slept with her. (She had purified herself from her monthly uncleanness.) Then she went back home. The woman conceived and sent word to David, saying, "I am pregnant." (2 Samuel 11:2–5)

David sinned by having a sexual relationship with the wife of Uriah, a loyal soldier in David's army, and then he sinned again when he tried to cover his sin by arranging the murder of Uriah. David ordered Joab, the leader of his army, to place Uriah at the front of the battle, knowing this would likely result in Uriah's death. His plan succeeded, and once Uriah was dead, David took Bathsheba for his wife. Later, the Lord sent the prophet Nathan to confront David about his sin.

> Then Nathan said to David, "You are the man! This is what the Lord, the God of Israel, says: 'I anointed you king over Israel, and I delivered you from the hand of Saul. I gave your master's house to you, and your master's wives into your arms. I gave you all Israel and Judah. And if all this had been too little, I would have given you even more. Why did you despise the word of the Lord by doing what is evil in his eyes? You struck down Uriah the Hittite with the sword and took his wife to be your own. You killed him with the sword of the Ammonites. Now, therefore, the sword will never depart from your house, because you despised me and took the wife of Uriah the Hittite to be your own…. Then David said to Nathan, "I have sinned against the LORD." Nathan replied, "The LORD has taken away your sin. You are not going to die." (2 Samuel 12:7–10, 13)

David comes to the realization of his sinful behavior and is filled with godly sorrow. Psalm 51 reveals David's godly sorrow and repentant heart. The Lord forgave David of this sin because the Lord saw his heart filled with godly sorrow; however, David did suffer worldly consequences because of his sin.

> For I know my transgressions, and my sin is always before me. Against you, you only, have I sinned and done what is evil in your sight; so you are right in your verdict and justified when you judge. (Psalm 51:3-4)

King Saul also sinned against God. He did not follow God's instructions in destroying the Amalekites, and he built a memorial to glorify himself instead of giving God the glory.

> Then the word of the LORD came to Samuel: "I regret that I have made Saul king, because he has turned away from me and has not carried out my instructions." Samuel was angry, and he cried out to the LORD all that night. Early in the morning Samuel got up and went to meet Saul, but he was told, "Saul has gone to Carmel. There he has set up a monument in his own honor and has turned and gone on down to Gilgal… For rebellion is like the sin of divination, and arrogance like the evil of idolatry. Because you have rejected the word of the LORD, he has rejected you as king." Then Saul said to Samuel, "I have sinned. I violated the LORD's command and your instructions. I was afraid of the men and so I gave in to them." (1 Samuel 15:10–12, 23–24)

Saul admitted he had sinned, but did he have godly sorrow? He was attempting to justify his sin by stating he feared his men. Attempting to justify our sinful behavior can become an easy habit because the longer we think about something, we will find a way to justify it.

17

> Saul replied, "I have sinned. But please honor me before the elders of my
> people and before Israel; come back with me, so that I may worship the LORD
> your God." (1 Samuel 15:30)

Saul wanted forgiveness so God would support him as the king of Israel but not because of any godly sorrow. Saul became filled with pride and wanted God's help for his own personal glory.

> He inquired of the LORD, but the LORD did not answer him by dreams or Urim
> or prophets. (1 Samuel 28:6)

The Lord was no longer with Saul because he did not have godly sorrow and a repentant heart. God is eager to forgive our sins when we have godly sorrow and a repentant heart. No sin is too big for God's forgiveness.

> Godly sorrow brings repentance that leads to salvation and leaves no regret,
> but worldly sorrow brings death. (2 Corinthians 7:10)

> God opposes the proud but shows favor to the humble. (James 4:6)

Explain the difference between worldly sorrow and godly sorrow.

_____

_____

_____

God did not forgive Saul because of his prideful heart. Can you identify any prideful behavior in your life?

_____

_____

_____

The Cost of Our Forgiveness

God's ultimate love and forgiveness is seen through the sacrifice of Jesus, the Son of God.

> But God demonstrates his own love for us in this: While we were still sinners,
> Christ died for us. (Romans 5:8)

God paid the debt for our sins through his own Son while we were still in our sinful state. In the garden of Gethsemane, Jesus prayed to the Lord,

> "Father, if you are willing, take this cup from me; yet not my will, but yours
> be done." An angel from heaven appeared to him and strengthened him. And

being in anguish, he prayed more earnestly, and his sweat was like drops of blood falling to the ground. (Luke 22:42–44)

Christ was asking the Father if there was another way to redeem mankind. The Father sent an angel to comfort him but did not change the path set before him. So Christ went to the cross, revealing the perfect love he and the Father have for you and me.

Jesus said, "Father, forgive them, for they do not know what they are doing." And they divided up his clothes by casting lots. (Luke 23:34)

Christ was showing love and a forgiving heart to the ones who were crucifying him. God is love, and his forgiveness is demonstrated by his grace and mercy offered to us through Christ. God has provided the perfect sacrifice to take the punishment for our sins, Jesus Christ his Son. We have forgiveness of past, present, and future sins, and God chooses to remember our sins no longer.

I, even I, am he who blots out your transgressions, for my own sake, and remembers your sins no more. (Isaiah 43:25)

God's forgiveness is for those who repent, believe, accept Jesus Christ as their Savior, and have received the Holy Spirit. Our love for God gives us a repentant heart with godly sorrow, which leads us to seek forgiveness. With a repentant heart, we seek to change from our sinful ways and walk closer with the Lord.

How can knowing God forgives you help you to forgive others?

_____
_____
_____

What gave Jesus the strength to endure flogging and death on the cross?

_____
_____
_____

Forgiveness of Self

Therefore, there is now no condemnation for those who are in Christ Jesus. (Romans 8:1)

When you ask God for forgiveness with a repentant heart and are forgiven, do you struggle with guilt or shame? God paid the ultimate price for our sins and chooses to remember them no more because he wants us to be free in Christ, free to serve him through loving obedience to his pleasing and perfect will. He wants us to accept his love and forgiveness so he can bless us through this life and into eternity, and he can't do that if we condemn ourselves for sins he has forgiven. We could be condemning ourselves to an eternity without God if we do not except his forgiveness.

Love "keeps no record of wrongs" (1 Corinthians 13:5). If you cannot forgive yourself, seek God's unconditional love to fill your heart. Unforgiveness for ourselves or for others is toxic to us and can destroy us spiritually and can even hurt our mental and physical health. Forgiveness frees the heart to receive God's love, peace, and joy.

"There is no lasting joy in forgiveness if it doesn't include forgiving yourself … It is as wrong as not forgiving others, because God loves us just as much as He loves others; He will be just as unhappy when we don't forgive ourselves as when we hold a grudge against others. Put simply, we matter to God. He wants our lives to be filled with joy," said former pastor and founder of R. T. Kendall Ministries, R. T. Kendall.[10]

Explain why God wants us to have a heart of forgiveness.

_____

_____

_____

Explain how unconditional love leads to a repentant heart.

_____

_____

_____

Forgiveness of Others

Just as God has forgiven our sins and remembers them no more, we are to forgive others who have sinned against us. Read the Scriptures on how much God loves you and the price he paid for you to be forgiven. God loves us, and the center of that love is forgiveness through Christ. Know that when you forgive others, God is forgiving you.

> For if you forgive other people when they sin against you, your heavenly Father will also forgive you. But if you do not forgive others their sins, your Father will not forgive your sins. (Matthew 6:14–15)

We forgive others to free ourselves, giving our anger and resentful heart to God and turning the person over to God. An unforgiving heart is toxic to mind, body, and soul while a forgiving heart brings peace and health.

When we carry unforgiveness and bitterness, explain how it can affect all our relationships.

_____

_____

_____

How does forgiveness free our hearts?

_____

_____

_____

Summary

God sacrificed his own Son for our sins and sends the Holy Spirit to live in us. This is what God did to redeem us and reflects how much he loves us, wants a close, loving relationship with us, and for us to live with him for all eternity. This reveals the love God has for you and me, and he expects us to reflect his love in us by having a forgiving heart. "Love keeps no records of wrong" (1 Corinthians 13:5), and if we do not forgive our brother, God will not forgive us (Matthew 6:15). This is the seriousness God has revealed to us about having unconditional love and a forgiving heart. If God can sacrifice his Son for our sins, for our sinful life, he certainly expects us to have forgiveness for self and for others. Unforgiveness in our hearts is poison to our soul, mind, and health. Unforgiveness mainly hurts one person, self. Forgiveness frees a hurting heart and brings peace and comfort.

Lesson 4: The Holy Spirit

Introduction

The Holy Spirit is the third person of the Trinity: Father, Son, and Spirit. When Christ returned to heaven, he asked the Father to send the Holy Spirit to believers. This demonstrates God's love because not only did Christ take the punishment for our sins, he sent the Holy Spirit to live in us. The Holy Spirit is our connection to God, and "no one knows the thoughts of God except the Spirit of God" (1 Corinthians 2:11). It is the Holy Spirit who changes our heart and enables us to walk with the Lord by providing his divine power and authority into our lives. The fruit of the Holy Spirit provides what we have been looking for but never find in the world.

This lesson will attempt to convey the blessing it is that God sent the person of the Holy Spirit to live in his children. The goal is to know that the Spirit of God lives in us and to live each day through the love and power of the Spirit. We will discuss how we receive the Holy Spirit, the tasks of the Spirit, the fruit of the Spirit, and living in the Spirit.

Receiving the Holy Spirit

> If you love me, keep my commands. And I will ask the Father, and he will give you another Advocate to help you and be with you forever—the Spirit of truth. The world cannot accept him, because it neither sees him nor knows him. But you know him, for he lives with you and will be in you. (John 14:15–17)

From this verse, we see that the Holy Spirit is referred to as "he," therefore the Holy Spirit is a person and he lives in the believer.

> And you also were included in Christ when you heard the message of truth, the gospel of your salvation. When you believed, you were marked in him with a seal, the promised Holy Spirit, who is a deposit guaranteeing our inheritance until the redemption of those who are God's possession—to the praise of his glory. (Ephesians 1:13–14)

The key requirement for receiving the Holy Spirit is to believe in your heart that Jesus Christ is your Savior and know that the Holy Spirit is your deposit guaranteeing eternal life. Since we live out of our heart, believing in our heart will give us the desire to repent and follow Christ as our Lord.

> Peter replied, "Repent and be baptized, every one of you, in the name of Jesus Christ for the forgiveness of your sins. And you will receive the gift of the Holy Spirit." (Acts 2:38)

> If you declare with your mouth, "Jesus is Lord," and believe in your heart that God raised him from the dead, you will be saved. (Romans 10:9)

We are to believe in our heart, not just in our mind. We always do what we believe, and if we believe in our heart that Christ is the Savior, it will be reflected in our lives. The conditions to receiving the Holy Spirit are to believe, accept Christ as Lord of your life, have a repentant heart, followed by baptism.

> For it is by grace you have been saved, through faith—and this is not from yourselves, it is the gift of God. (Ephesians 2:8)

We are saved by grace through faith, which is a gift of God. We live by faith, trusting the Lord's guidance through living in the realm of the Holy Spirit. We show our love for God by trusting him and walking in obedience to his commands.

> You, however, are not in the realm of the flesh but are in the realm of the Spirit, if indeed the Spirit of God lives in you. And if anyone does not have the Spirit of Christ, they do not belong to Christ. (Romans 8:9)

To receive the Holy Spirit, we must first believe. How do we attain this belief in God and his Word?

_____

_____

_____

Describe what it means to "believe in your heart."

_____

_____

_____

Tasks of the Holy Spirit

> In the same way, the Spirit helps us in our weakness. We do not know what we ought to pray for, but the Spirit himself intercedes for us through wordless groans. And he who searches our hearts knows the mind of the Spirit, because the Spirit intercedes for God's people in accordance with the will of God. (Romans 8:26–27)

The Holy Spirit intercedes with our prayers to present them perfectly to the Lord, and he intercedes in our ministry to keep us in the will of God.

> But the Advocate, the Holy Spirit, whom the Father will send in my name, will teach you all things and will remind you of everything I have said to you. (John 14:26)

The Spirit will teach us all things and remind us of Jesus's teaching. Many times in my ministry, whether preaching, teaching, or mentoring, I ask the Lord for the words applicable in the situation. If I listen with patience, the Spirit provides direction.

> These are the things God has revealed to us through his Spirit. The Spirit searches all things, even the deep things of God. For who knows a person's thoughts except their own spirit within them? In the same way no one knows the thoughts of God except the Spirit of God. What we have received is not the spirit of the world, but the Spirit who is from God, so that we may understand what God has freely given us. This is what we speak, not in words taught us by human wisdom but in words taught by the Spirit, explaining spiritual realities with Spirit-taught words. The person without the Spirit does not accept the things that come from the Spirit of God but considers them foolishness, and cannot understand them because they are discerned only through the Spirit. (1 Corinthians 2:10–14)

It is through the Holy Spirit that we understand the ways of God. It is the Spirit who makes God's Word alive to us, sharper than a two-edge sword (Hebrews 4:12). The Word is Spiritually discerned, and the Spirit speaks only what he hears from God (John 16:13). The more we understand God's Word, the more we can recognize the Holy Spirit.

> But when he, the Spirit of truth, comes, he will guide you into all the truth. He will not speak on his own; he will speak only what he hears, and he will tell you what is yet to come. (John 16:13)

The Holy Spirit will convict us when we sin, letting us know when our thoughts, words, and actions are against the truth of God's Word. Remember, conviction is correction that brings us in line with the will of God, thereby bringing us closer to God and enabling us to make godly wise decisions. Without conviction from the Holy Spirit, we would never mature as Christians. Sometimes we would not be aware that we are leaning toward sin without the Holy Spirit's conviction.

God gives us the Holy Spirit to seal our eternal life, understand the ways of God, intercede in our prayers and in our ministry, and convict us when we drift into sin.

> Jesus replied, "If anyone loves me, he will obey my teaching. My Father will love yhrm, and we will come to him and make our home with them." (John 14:23)

This is the love that God has for us, that the Father and the Son will come and make their home with us: Father, Son, and Spirit. We are indeed in the family of God and have started living our eternal life here on earth.

Explain how through the Holy Spirit God's Word comes alive.

_____

_____

_____

How can the Holy Spirit "tell you what is yet to come"?

_____

_____

_____

Fruit of the Holy Spirit

> But the fruit of the Spirit is love, joy, peace, patience, kindness, goodness, faithfulness, gentleness and self-control. (Galatians 5:22–23)

The fruit of the Holy Spirit sustains us through the trials and tribulations of this worldly life. We are created to live for eternity with God, and our eternal soul seeks this heavenly life. However, God knows we will face hardships in this life and the world cannot bring the life our soul seeks. Therefore, God brings heaven to us in the form of the indwelling Holy Spirit, bringing us eternal love, peace, and joy to satisfy our eternal soul. The Holy Spirit brings life to our soul (John 6:63).

The fruit of the Holy Spirit is love and all the other fruit is characteristics of God's love. During the course of your walk with the Lord, you will mature in Christ and the fruit of the Spirit will become stronger in your life. The fruit never goes away because it is spiritual and the Spirit is always with us. The more we are in the Spirit, showing spiritual fruit to others, the more we experience the fruit.

> I am the vine; you are the branches. If you remain in me and I in you, you will bear much fruit; apart from me you can do nothing. (John 15:5)

Without the Holy Spirit, we are powerless to change and become the persons God created us to be. Charles Stanley says,

> The power of the Holy Spirit is the divine authority and energy that God releases into the life of every one of his children in order that we might live a godly and fruitful life. The Word tells us that we become "clothed from on high" by this power—it envelops us, not only covering us and protecting us from the influences of the devil, but also enabling us to demonstrate the likeness of Christ. The Holy Spirit covers us in such a way that we bear both the fruit of his character and the demonstration of his presence wherever we go.[11]

Explain how the Holy Spirit brings life to our soul.

_____
_____
_____

Which fruit of the Holy Spirit gives you the most trouble?

_____
_____
_____

Living in the Spirit

The Holy Spirit speaks the Word of God. The more we understand the Word, the more we will hear the Holy Spirit. The Spirit will convict us when we are going in the wrong direction and will bring God's Word to us when we need it. The more we commune with God through the Spirit, the more we will be prompted by the Spirit. A typical example occurred when I was walking downtown here in Frederick, Maryland, asking the Lord to open my eyes to minister to anyone he puts in my path. As I was walking, I was prompted to go straight at the intersection, which was unusual because I always go right. I followed the overpowering urge, and a few minutes later, I heard a voice behind me call my name. I turned around and saw a gentleman who used to be in my prison Bible class. We had lunch, and that evening I took him to Celebrate Recovery with me. If I hadn't been communing with God but instead lost in my own thoughts, this opportunity to minister would probably never have happened.

When we live in the Spirit, we can recognize the Spirit working in our life. The fruit of the Spirit starts to become our new nature, the godly nature. Love from God is reflected to others in the form of kindness, gentleness, patience, faithfulness, and self-control, and the peace and joy from the Spirit is now revealed in our life. We now care for others with compassion, encouraging, helping, and praying for them, and our godly nature is evident as we become more other-focused. When God's love through the Spirit captures our heart, we begin to see people as God sees them and we develop the desire to help others, both in their physical needs and their spiritual needs. The more love we give by ministering to others, the more love our hearts can receive from God, making us more Christlike.

The Holy Spirit gives us the power to speak and teach his Word with boldness and authority. We can stand strong in God's truth, presenting his truth in love. You can recognize a person guided by the Spirit because he or she speaks boldly because they speak the truth from God. The Holy Spirit empowers and energizes us to witness Christ to others.

> God hath not given us the spirit of fear; but of power, and of love, and of a sound mind. (2 Timothy 1:7, KJV)

The Holy Spirit changes us by renewing our mind and filling our heart with God's love. As we come to know God's perfect love for us, our trust in God gets stronger until our heart seeks God's will. When we have surrendered to God's love, our will becomes God's will, and for the first time in our life, we are in control through the power of the Holy Spirit. At this point in our walk, we are overcoming the world with our mind and emotions under control of the Holy Spirit.

> "I have told you these things, so that in me you may have peace. In this world you will have trouble. But take heart! I have overcome the world. (John 16:33)

> For everyone born of God overcomes the world. (1 John 5:4)

The following is a quote from A.W. Tozer in *The Pursuit of God,* which describes what it means to truly walk in the Spirit:

> Many have found the secret of which I speak and, without giving much thought to what is going on within them, constantly practice this habit of inwardly gazing upon God. They know that something inside their hearts sees God. Even when they are compelled to withdraw their conscious minds attention in order to engage in earthly affairs, there is within them a secret communion always going on. Let their attention but be released for a moment from necessary business and flies at once to God again. This has been the testimony of many Christians, from whom or how many I cannot know.[12]

First Thessalonians 5:17 commands, "Pray continually." Those who live in the Spirit communing with the Lord almost constantly have learned to sense the presence of the Holy Spirit's connection to God.

Describe what it means to "overcome the world."

_____

_____

_____

The quote from Tozer states that "a secret communion always going on." Can you explain this secret communion?

_____

_____

_____

Summary

The Holy Spirit will change us from our worldly sinful nature to Christlike nature, the mind of Christ. The Spirit will fill our heart with God's love, and as we reflect that love to others, God's love in us grows stronger. The love from God received in the Spirit gives us strength and casts away our fear as we trust God's perfect love. When we truly experience patience and love from the Spirit, we will obtain more godly wisdom as we become quick to listen and slow to speak (James 1:19). When we live by the Spirit, we walk in godly wisdom, make wise decisions, and have a mind of love, hope, peace, and joy. As you go through your day, seek to be aware that the Spirit of God lives in you, whose purpose is to guide you through each day trusting God, and with your heart comforted by the fruit of the Spirit.

Lesson 5: Our New Identity

Introduction

God gives us a new identity when we accept Christ as our Savior and when we are filled with the Holy Spirit. No one can take this identity from us, although sometimes Christians forget who they are in Christ. Our identity is closely related to our divine purpose; for example, an auto mechanic describes a person who repairs cars. Likewise, our godly identity describes us as a servant of the Most High God. When we embrace our God-given purpose in our heart, we will live confidently, trusting that God will fulfill the work he has begun in us.

In this lesson, we will look at Scriptures that define our new identity, see why God gives us this new identity, and learn how it is essential in our daily ministry. We will stress the importance of being aware of our new identity because it has a major influence in our Christian life.

Our New Identity

We will first look at the new identity that God gives us after we accept Christ.

> Therefore, if anyone is in Christ, the new creation has come: The old has gone, the new is here! (2 Corinthians 5:17)

> For you have been born again, not of perishable seed, but of imperishable, through the living and enduring word of God. (1 Peter 1:23)

When we welcome Christ into our lives, we are made a new creation, born of God. Those are powerful words that God uses to describe the person we become when we accept Christ and receive the Holy Spirit. The longer we walk with the Lord, the more we realize we are a new creation, born of God, and the person God created us to be comes to life.

> The Spirit you received does not make you slaves, so that you live in fear again; rather, the Spirit you received brought about your adoption to sonship. And by him we cry, "Abba, Father." The Spirit himself testifies with our spirit that we

are God's children. Now if we are children, then we are heirs—heirs of God and co-heirs with Christ, if indeed we share in his sufferings in order that we may also share in his glory. (Romans 8:15–17)

We can compare our role as children in God's family to the children in our own family. We love and care for our children; we bless, protect, guide, support, and discipline them. We love all the children in the neighborhood, but we don't treat them like our own. We belong to God, and he sees us and blesses us as his children. We receive his grace, and he is our perfect Father, guiding us through life with his perfect will.

But he gives us more grace. That is why Scripture says: "God opposes the proud but shows favor to the humble." (James 4:6)

God loves everybody, but he doesn't treat everyone the same. When we accept Christ and live in God's family, we receive his grace, but he opposes those who refuse Christ. God opposed the Israelites when they sinned by worshipping idols. God stepped back and stopped protecting them, leaving them to their sinful ways, which led them to their fall and captivity by their enemies. The Israelites then ran back to God with a repentant heart and he took them back. That is the power of God's love, as seen through his forgiveness.

But you are a chosen people, a royal priesthood, a holy nation, God's special possession, that you may declare the praises of him who called you out of darkness into his wonderful light. (1 Peter 2:9)

Here Peter extends our identity to that of a chosen race, a royal priesthood, a holy nation, people for his own possession. We may not always feel like we are part of the royal priesthood, but we are. It's not based on feelings; it's based on truth.

Our new identity tells us that we belong to God, that we are his possession. God's love is so powerful that he fills us with his Spirit and sees us as his children. He wants us to know the truth and trust him, to understand that we are already saved and that his promise of eternal life has already started. We are secure in the righteous right hand of God (Isaiah 41:10), and we will someday cross over into the heavenly kingdom and into the glorious presence of the Father and the Son. We are in God's family now and forever.

How can our God-given identity give us security in this life?

_____

_____

_____

How is God's love for us demonstrated by the new identity he gives us?

_____

_____

_____

Our New Self-Worth

> But God demonstrates his own love for us in this; while we were still sinners,
> Christ died for us. (Romans 5:8)

When we accept Christ as our Savior and receive the Holy Spirit, God gives us a new identity; he calls us his children, heirs, priests, and saints. Why do you think God gives us this high-standing identity? It reveals his love for us and our importance to him. This new identity is exclusively ours from God, and no one and nothing can take it from us, for it gives us a divine self-worth. There is no higher identity or self-worth than what God gives us, and since it is all from God, it makes us humble and secure because it is nothing we produced ourselves. Now we can minister to the world without pride or trying to prove ourselves to others. We can now be known by our love.

It wasn't until Christ gave me a new identity that for the first time I had self-worth. Previously, my self-worth was based on my successes, education, job title, and triathlon performance. I had a prideful identity and yet still felt inferior in many situations. Now walking with Christ, belonging to and loved by God, I have a strong self-worth in Christ that is not prideful. Our self-worth in Christ is given to us by Christ, and our self-worth is really our worship to God for giving us a divine identity. When our self-worth truly comes from our God-given identity, it makes us humble because we know who we are in Christ. We are now secure and can minister to everyone, even to those who might respond to us aggressively. We can respond with God's love and godly wisdom because our God-given identity can remove our defensive behavior.

Rick Warren, author of *The Purpose Driven Life*, states,

> Bringing enjoyment to God, living for his pleasure, is the first purpose of your life. When you fully understand this truth, you never again have a problem with feeling insignificant. It proves your worth. If you are *that* important to God, and he considers you valuable enough to keep with him for eternity, what greater significance could you have? You are a child of God, and you bring pleasure to God like nothing else he has ever created. [13]

Explain how our new identity in Christ gives us high self-worth and how it makes us humble.

_____

_____

_____

Explain how we can control our defensive behavior when we know our God-given identity.

_____

_____

_____

Our New Purpose

> I have been crucified with Christ and I no longer live, but Christ lives in me.
> The life I now live in the body, I live by faith in the Son of God, who loved me
> and gave himself for me. (Galatians 2:20)

The apostle Paul had his identity in Christ and in the person of the Holy Spirit. Through the Holy Spirit, God is molding us to have the mind of Christ, to be made in likeness to his Son. Christian means "Christlike." The more Christlike we become, the more we will live our God-given identity.

> I became a servant of this gospel by the gift of God's grace given me through
> the working of his power. Although I am less than the least of all Lord's people,
> this grace was given me: to preach to the Gentiles the boundless riches of
> Christ. (Ephesians 3:7–8)

Christ chose Paul to be the apostle to the Gentiles, and Paul lived his life fulfilling his commission from Christ. He embraced his identity in Christ and security as a child of God and became a servant of Christ, ministering to the Gentiles and establishing churches. When we embrace our God-given identity, we will embrace our God-given purpose. Our identity is in Christ and our life is Christ.

If Paul did not have his identity in Christ as a child of God, how could he have lived the life we read about? If we do not embrace our new identity from God, how can we truly be a servant of the Lord? When we embrace our God-given identity, it defines who we are, a new creation filled with God's love. Our new identity gives us assurance of membership in God's family, that God is always with us, and of eternal life with God.

It is through our new identity that we live our God-given purpose. I ask God to let me always be aware of my divine purpose for existence and that I can continually know this, just as I know I continually exist. God answered those prayers, and today I am glad to say I always know my divine purpose: to be Christlike, pointing people to Christ by my attitude and actions. Learning how to do this is a lifelong task. Life has divine meaning and purpose when we are aware of our new identity, living for Christ, and living life to the full (John 10:10).

If we always know our God-given purpose, the reason we exist, how can it change our life?

_____

_____

_____

Describe your God-given identity.

_____

_____

_____

Our New Perseverance

> I have worked much harder, been in prison more frequently, been flogged more severely, and been exposed to death again and again. Five times I received from the Jews the forty lashes minus one. Three times I was beaten with rods, once I was pelted with stones, three times I was shipwrecked, I spent a night and a day in the open sea, I have been constantly on the move. I have been in danger from rivers, in danger from bandits, in danger from my fellow Jews, in danger from Gentiles; in danger in the city, in danger in the country, in danger at sea; and in danger from false believers. I have labored and toiled and have often gone without sleep; I have known hunger and thirst and have often gone without food; I have been cold and naked. Besides everything else, I face daily the pressure of my concern for all the churches. Who is weak, and I do not feel weak? Who is led into sin, and I do not inwardly burn? (2 Corinthians 11:23–29)

Paul's identity in Christ and his eternal life in God's family gave him the motivation and perseverance to fulfill his purpose with the strength, courage, and wisdom given to him by God. When we live for our eternal life and divine purpose, and embrace our godly identity, we will have strength and endurance to survive the trials and tribulations of life.

> I eagerly expect and hope that I will in no way be ashamed, but will have sufficient courage so that now as always Christ will be exalted in my body, whether by life or by death. For to me, to live is Christ and to die is gain. If I am to go on living in the body, this will mean fruitful labor for me. Yet what shall I choose? I do not know! I am torn between the two: I desire to depart and be with Christ, which is better by far; but it is more necessary for you that I remain

in the body. Convinced of this, I know that I will remain, and I will continue with all of you for your progress and joy in the faith. (Philippians 1:20–25)

If Paul did not have his identity in Christ as a child of God, how could he say, "to live is Christ and to die is gain"? If we do not embrace our new identity in God, how can we truly endure as a servant of the Lord?

How can our God-given identity give us the perseverance we need in this life?

_____

_____

_____

What does our God-given identity do for us when trouble comes?

_____

_____

_____

Our New Home

"For they are not of the world any more than I am of the world" (John 17:14). This is from Christ's prayer shortly before he went to the cross. He is stating that his apostles are not of the world, even though they live in the world. It is the same for us. Filled with the Holy Spirit and destined for eternal life with the Father and the Son, we are not of the world. We will never forget this if we realize who we are in Christ by our new God-given identity because it points to our heavenly home.

> But our citizenship is in heaven. And we eagerly await a Savior from there, the Lord Jesus Christ, who, by the power that enables him to bring everything under his control, will transform our lowly bodies so that they will be like his glorious body. (Philippians 3:20-21)

Although we live in this world with the indwelling Holy Spirit, our citizenship is in heaven. I recently asked the men in my Bible class at the local prison, "Is this prison your home?" They all agreed their home was outside the prison and their stay in prison was temporary. Same for us; this world is not our home and our stay is temporary, for our citizenship is in heaven. Christ said, "My Father's house has many rooms; if that were not so, would I have told you that I am going there to prepare a place for you? And if I go and prepare a place for you, I will come back and take you to be with me that you also may be where I am. You know the way to the place where I am going" (John 14:1–4). The Holy Spirit is our deposit for eternal life.

Explain how knowing our God-given identity can help us to be mindful of our eternal life.

_____

_____

_____

Explain how our decisions today have eternal consequences.

_____

_____

_____

Summary

God's love is seen by the new identity he gives us, identifying that we are in his family and belong to him. When we embrace our God-given identity, it defines who we are, a new creation filled with God's love. This will give us a divine purpose and strength to endure this life, knowing God is always with us and has a permanent home for us. If we walk each day knowing who we are in Christ, it will give us security and keep us living in the Spirit where love, peace, and joy are found. This gives us a divine reason for our existence, pointing people to Christ, which becomes fulfilling to us because that is what we are created to do—to receive and reflect God's love to others: family, God's family, strangers, and even our enemies.

The goal of this lesson is to know in our hearts our God-given identity and to let this identity instill our purpose in our hearts and the reason we exist. Without knowing this in our hearts, it will be difficult to walk in the Spirit serving the Lord as we go through each day. Our identity defines who we are, and we live our identity. If we embrace our God-given identity, we live for Christ.

Lesson 6: Family of God

Introduction

From the previous lessons, we learned that God has given us the Holy Spirit and has given us a new identity. Now we will see that he has brought us into his divine family, the family of God. Being in the family of God can give us a very secure feeling if we understand in our heart the love, blessings, and protection that God gives his children. We are citizens of God's family and members of his household, which implies we have started our eternal life even though we still live in the flesh.

Being in God's family gives us a feeling of security, peace, and purpose. However, living in God's family can easily be forgotten as we go through our busy days. The goal of this lesson is to help us know in our heart that we are in God's family, that we are his children and heirs. We will look at what Scripture says about the family of God, the holiness of God's family, and the blessings in the family of God.

God's Family

Living in God's family with our new identity, we become secure and humble and receive God's grace. We have God's perfect forgiveness because we walk with a repentant heart seeking to overcome our sinful behavior and asking God for forgiveness when we fall short. God said in Isaiah 43:25 that God blots out our transgressions and remembers our sins no more. God's grace is his favor as he leads those in his family through life, and Scripture says he also goes before us (Deuteronomy 31:8).

> God opposes the proud but shows favor to the humble. (James 4:6)

> For we know that if the earthly tent we live in is destroyed, we have a building from God, an eternal house in heaven, not built by human hands. Meanwhile we groan, longing to be clothed instead with our heavenly dwelling, because when we are clothed, we will not be found naked. For while we are in this tent, we groan and are burdened, because we do not wish to be unclothed but to be clothed instead with our heavenly dwelling, so that what is mortal may be

swallowed up by life. Now the one who has fashioned us for this very purpose is God, who has given us the Spirit as a deposit, guaranteeing what is to come. (2 Corinthians 5:1–5)

The people in the family of God are heaven-bound and eternally minded, waiting for their home in heaven. When we are aware that we are in the family of God, it helps us be eternally minded, thereby encouraging us in this life by knowing our perseverance is temporary. When we go through the trials and tribulation of this life, the family of God is there to support us. Our close Christian brothers and sisters will walk with us, encourage us, support us, and reveal God's love to us. God created us for relationships, and when our Christian friends in God's family support us, God is also supporting us with his divine love, power, and comfort.

Describe the difference between a Christian friend and a non-Christian friend.

_____

_____

_____

Describe what being in the family of God means to you.

_____

_____

_____

A Holy Nation

But you are a chosen people, a royal priesthood, a holy nation, God's special possession, that you may declare the praises of him who called you out of darkness into his wonderful light. (1 Peter 2:9)

The family of God consists of people who are a royal priesthood, a holy nation, and people who belong to God. If we truly know what it means to belong to God, it can change our lives, knowing we will be with God now and forever. This shows his perfect love for us and gives us security, knowing God will carry us through this life into heaven with him.

But just as he who called you is holy, so be holy in all you do; for it is written: "Be holy, because I am holy." (1 Peter 1:15–16)

Holy means to be set apart, just as God is holy. We are set apart because there is none who is his equal; no one is like God. We are in the family of God, and we are holy because we walk with God, which makes us different from people who walk the way of the world. Knowing our purpose and knowing we live in the family of God can help us remain holy and can help keep Satan from pulling us into the sinful ways of the world.

We are royal priests, which makes us holy. In the Old Testament, people worshipped God at the temple and the priests were assigned to the temple to perform the religious duties. Since Christ, we have become the earthly temple because God dwells in us through the Holy Spirit. Your body is now the temple and you are the priest. We are God's elect, his priests who serve him in his temples here on earth.

> You also are living stones that are being built into a spiritual house; moreover, you are a holy priesthood who are to offer spiritual sacrifices that are acceptable to the Father through Jesus Christ. (1 Peter 2:5)

What does it mean that we each are a spiritual house?

_____

_____

_____

Describe an incident that kept you from being holy.

_____

_____

_____

The Church

The Church is represented as the bride of Christ with Christ as the bridegroom. It was customary in biblical times to have a betrothal period after the engagement that the bride and the groom were separated until the wedding. The bride was to remain faithful to the groom during this time. Likewise, the church is to remain faithful until Christ returns for the wedding ceremony.

> Let us rejoice and be glad and give him glory! For the wedding of the Lamb has come, and his bride has made herself ready. (Revelation 19:7)

God's family is the church, and the head of the church is Christ. The church meets together so God's people can encourage one another through God's love and worship, praise God, and study his Word. The church can be very powerful when God's love is displayed through the people. We need our brothers and sisters in the church to help us remain faithful to Christ so we will be ready for the wedding ceremony when Christ returns. The church is our family of brothers and sisters for all eternity.

> And let us consider how we may spur one another on toward love and good deeds, not giving up meeting together, as some are in the habit of doing, but encouraging one another—and all the more as you see the Day approaching. (Hebrews 10:24–25)

The church is where we receive God's love, encouragement, and strength to go out into the world and minister to people. I personally know that without my church family and close Christian brothers and sisters, I would not be walking with the Lord today. Part of what the Lord has called me to do each week consists of prison ministry and lay counseling men who are trying to overcome addictions. This sometimes takes a toll both emotionally and physically, but every Sunday morning I am renewed and motivated by God's love and strength through the brothers and sisters in the church. The following verse captures my feelings during these times:

> But those who hope in the LORD will renew their strength. They will soar on wings like eagles; they will run and not grow weary, they will walk and not be faint. (Isaiah 40:31)

Our close brothers and sisters in God's family, the church, will hold us accountable with love and encouragement. Whenever we drift into sin, our godly family will gently lead us back into God's grace, and when we are wrestling with sin, our godly family will pray and encourage us to victory.

> Therefore confess your sins to each other and pray for each other so that you may be healed. The prayer of a righteous person is powerful and effective. (James 5:16)

If we confess our sins to a close Christian friend, someone in the church in the family of God, we receive understanding, support, love, and forgiveness. When we confess our sins and receive love and support from our Christian friend, it helps us to repent and heal. Confessing our sins to a close Christian friend can heal us from guilt, shame, and self-condemnation.

> Consequently, you are no longer foreigners and strangers, but fellow citizens with God's people and also members of his household, built on the foundation of the apostles and prophets, with Christ Jesus himself as the chief cornerstone. (Ephesians 2:19–20)

I was recently traveling and visited a church that accepted me like family. The members went the extra mile to make me feel at home. I was invited to lunch by a couple and spent the day with them. They were godly people who made me feel like family as we discussed things of God. After church that evening, another couple invited me to a restaurant for dinner, and we spent almost three hours discussing things related to our ministry. I was filled with God's love reflected by these people and was on a spiritual high all week. This is the power of the family of God, lifting us spiritually through the love from God.

How do we support our Christian brothers and sisters?

_____

_____

_____

What can you do to strengthen the church?

_____

_____

_____

Discipleship

A disciple in Jesus' day was someone who followed in the footsteps of the rabbi. Today, we are disciples of Christ and follow his footsteps to become Christlike. Christ said, "Whoever wants to be my disciple must deny themselves and take up their cross and follow me" (Matthew 16:24). The church is the ideal place to learn about discipleship, Bible study to learn more about Christ, and learn from others about being a disciple. When I first gave my life to Christ, I teamed with a mature Christian as we served the Lord together helping the homeless, teaching in the prison, and becoming an active part of the church. "Calling the Twelve to him, he began to send them out two by two and gave them authority over impure spirits" (Mark 6:7). It is now eleven years later, and my brother has moved out of the area. It was that first year in the church that I began to learn to be a disciple and have been learning more every day from my church family and walking with the Lord. Discipleship is something that we continue to learn just as we continue to learn more about Christ and develop a closer relationship with him, which opens our heart to receive more of God's love. It's love that drives us to be disciples.

> By this everyone will know that you are my disciples, if you love one another.
> (John 13:35)

We are created to be disciples, to live by faith and follow Christ, enabling God to mold us to have the mind of Christ. "Discipleship isn't a program or an event; it's a way of life. It's not for a limited time, but for our whole life. Discipleship isn't for beginners alone; it's for all believers for every day of their life. Discipleship isn't just one of those things the church does; it is what the church does. It's not just part of the advancement of God's kingdom; the existence of serious disciples is the most important evidence of God's work on earth," said pastor and author Bill Hull. [14]

Give your understanding of Matthew 16:24, Then Jesus said to his disciples, "Whoever wants to be my disciple must deny themselves and take up their cross and follow me.

_____

_____

_____

Why do think Christ sent his apostles out two by two?

_____

_____

_____

The Cost of Discipleship

The following verses about being a disciple of Christ is one of the strongest soul-searching verses Jesus ever spoke:

> If anyone comes to me and does not hate father and mother, wife and children, brothers and sisters—yes, even their own life—such a person cannot be my disciple. And whoever does not carry their cross and follow me cannot be my disciple. (Luke 14:26–27)

These verses tell us the requirement for being a disciple of Christ. Christ is not saying that we literary hate our family, but we are to love God more than anyone or anything. When we love God more, we actually are filled with more of his love and able to love our family more. We are also to love God more than self, and this is demonstrated by those who are dying today because they will not deny Christ as their Lord.

In this world we will have trials and tribulations, and some of these trials will bring us hurt and pain. When we love the Lord more than anyone or anything, we will live for a divine purpose, and nothing in this world will stop us from fulfilling this purpose. We obtain incredible strength when we love the Lord more than others, giving us the ability to endure anything this world puts in our path. This love gives us the strength to endure death for our Lord, knowing our heavenly reward awaits us.

How does loving God more than anyone or anything help us in our Christian walk?

_____

_____

_____

Christians are dying every day for their faith in Christ by not denying Christ. What gives them the strength and courage to die for Christ?

_____

_____

_____

Summary

God created us for relationships. The first relationship is with the Father and the Son and then our family and our godly family. Our godly family is the church, our brothers and sisters for eternity. Through God's family, we gain strength and wisdom from God, enabling us to endure whatever Satan puts in our path. Through the church, we worship the Lord, have group Bible study, and receive and give God's love. The church family is our godly home in this sinful world.

If we try to walk alone without fellowship with others in God's family, we can find our spiritual life suffering. Just as the lion attacks the one straying from the herd, Satan is like a roaring lion and attacks those who stray from God's family. Christ's body is the church, and if we are not fellowshipping with God's people, encouraging, uplifting, and supporting others, are we part of the body? The more we give love, encouragement, and support to the church, the more we receive. We receive by giving.

If you are experiencing God's love in your church family, you are blessed. If you are not experiencing the blessings of being in the church, please seek a loving church where Christ can show his love for you and bless you through his family.

Lesson 7: Word of God

Introduction

The Bible is the Word of God, and it is how God reveals himself. Without his divine Word, we would never know God and his love for us or the reason we exist. We will briefly look at the Bible in terms of history, structure, and prophecy. We will review the importance of God's Word and how it becomes alive, helps us hear the Spirit, and can become a major part of our daily life. God places great emphasis on words; he created the universe from his words, reveals himself through his words, and says our words are important.

The Bible is one book we can read consistently all through our life and never stop receiving divine messages from God. It is where we are forever gaining more understanding of God by walking in obedience to his will and being in his Word. Obedience to his Word opens our mind and heart to receive the deep things of God. Charles Stanley says,

> The Lord's primary way of speaking to us today is through his Word. We already have the complete revelation of God. He doesn't need to add anything else to this Book. The revelation of God is the unfolding truth of God by God about Himself. It is the inspiration of the Holy Spirit, controlling the minds of men who penned the pages that make up the Bible. The Bible is the breath of God breathed upon those men that they might know the truth.[15]

Overview of the Bible

The Bible was written over a period of approximately fifteen hundred years and was written by forty authors with varying cultural and educational backgrounds. These authors came from three different continents—Asia, Africa, and Europe—and the Bible was written in three different languages—Hebrew, Aramaic, and Greek. Yet the sixty-six books of the Bible fit together perfectly with the constant theme of God's relationship to man and God's plan for man's salvation through Christ. Historical and architectural discoveries have constantly supported the accuracy of the Bible.[16]

The Bible consists of two parts, the Old Testament and the New Testament. The Old Testament is the covenant the Lord had with the nation Israel, and the New Testament is the covenant with all mankind through Christ our Savior.

Old Testament

God established the Israelite nation from one man, Abraham, and this nation was God's people. They were to worship and follow God so other nations would recognize the true God. Jesus's family lineage came from the Israelite nation through the house of David. The Old Testament covers the creation of the heavens and the earth, creation of man and woman, and the history of the nation Israel. From the Old Testament we see God's personality as he relates to the Israelites, Moses, Abraham, Saul, David, Jonah, and others, and God's attitude toward these people gives us an understanding of his attitude toward us.

There are thirty-nine books in the Old Testament, and they are divided into four major groups:

- Books of the Law: Genesis, Exodus, Leviticus, Numbers, and Deuteronomy
- Books of History: Joshua, Judges, Ruth, 1 and 2 Samuel, 1 and 2 Kings, 1 and 2 Chronicles, Ezra, Nehemiah, and Esther
- Books of Poetry and Wisdom: Job, Psalms, Proverbs, Ecclesiastes, Song of Solomon
- Books of Prophecy: Isaiah, Jeremiah, Lamentations, Ezekiel, Daniel, Hosea, Joel, Amos, Obadiah, Jonah, Micah, Nahum, Habakkuk, Zephaniah, Haggai, Zechariah, and Malachi

The Bible contains approximately twenty-five hundred prophecies and approximately two thousand have already been fulfilled.[17] These prophecies include God foretelling about the Israelite nation, prophecies concerning Jesus, and prophecies concerning the future. These prophecies are described in detail, and they were fulfilled in every detail. This can only happen by the divine knowledge of God. Below are a few New Testament Scriptures that show the fulfillment of the prophecy concerning Christ.

- But he was "pierced for our transgressions" (Isaiah 53:5); "But when they came to Jesus and found that he was already dead, they did not break his legs. Instead, one of the soldiers pierced Jesus' side with a spear, bringing a sudden flow of blood and water" (John 19:33–34).

- "He was assigned a grave with the wicked" (Isaiah 53.9); "When they came to the place called the Skull, they crucified him there, along with the criminals—one on his right, the other on his left" (Luke 23:33).

- "They divided my clothes among them and cast lots for my garments" (Psalm 22:18); "When the soldiers crucified Jesus, they took his clothes, dividing them into four shares, one for each of them, with the undergarment remaining. This garment was seamless, woven in one piece from top to bottom. 'Let's not tear it,' they said to one another. 'Let's decide by lot who will get it'" (John 19:23–24).

- "All who see me mock me; they hurl insults, shaking their heads: 'He trusts in the Lord; let the Lord rescue him'" (Psalm 22:7–8); "'He saved others,' they said, 'but he can't save himself! He's the king of Israel! Let him come down now from the cross, and we will believe in him. He trusts in God. Let God rescue him now if he wants him, for he said, 'I am the Son of God'" (Matthew 27:42–43).

The time period between the end of the Old Testament and the beginning of the New Testament is approximately four hundred years. During this period, there is no recording of God's words to the Israelites written in the Bible. Daniel prophesied about these four hundred years in Daniel 11.

The New Testament

The New Testament describes the birth of Jesus, his ministry, and his death by crucifixion. It relates the history of the early church and includes letters written to the church and other Christians. The New Testament is full of instructions on being saved by God's grace through Christ and living by faith through the indwelling Holy Spirit.

The New Testament consists of twenty-seven books divided into four divisions:

- Gospels: Matthew, Mark, Luke, and John
- Historical record of the early church: Acts
- Epistles: Romans; 1 and 2 Corinthians; Galatians; Ephesians; Philippians; Colossians; 1 and 2 Thessalonians; 1 and 2 Timothy; Titus; Philemon; Hebrews; James; 1 and 2 Peter; 1, 2, and 3 John; and Jude
- Prophecy: Revelation

The New Testament was written by eight authors who either walked with Jesus or walked with one of the apostles. Known authors of the New Testament are Matthew, Mark, Luke, John, Peter, Paul, James, and Jude. The author of Hebrews is unknown. Paul was converted to Christianity and became an apostle after meeting Christ on the road to Damascus (Acts 9:1–18). This occurred after Jesus ascended into heaven. James and Jude were half brothers of Jesus. Luke was a physician and was the only Gentile author of the New Testament. He was often with the apostle Paul during his missionary journeys and when Paul was in prison. Mark accompanied Paul on his first missionary journey, and according to history, he started the church in Alexandria. It is estimated that the New Testament was written between the years AD50 and AD95.

Why is it important to read and understand the Old Testament?

_____

_____

_____

Explain why the prophecies of the Bible always come true to the exact detail.

_____

_____

_____

The Word Is Alive

> For the word of God is alive and active. Sharper than any double-edged sword, it penetrates even to dividing soul and spirit, joints and marrow; it judges the thoughts and attitudes of the heart. (Hebrews 4:12)

> The Spirit searches all things, even the deep things of God. For who knows a person's thoughts except their own spirit within them? In the same way no one knows the thoughts of God except the Spirit of God. What we have received is not the spirit of the world, but the Spirit who is from God, so that we may understand what God has freely given us. This is what we speak, not in words taught us by human wisdom but in words taught by the Spirit, explaining spiritual realities with Spirit-taught words. The person without the Spirit does not accept the things that come from the Spirit of God but considers them foolishness, and cannot understand them because they are discerned only through the Spirit. (1 Corinthians 2:10–14)

This Scripture states that "no one knows the thoughts of God except the Spirit of God" and "they are discerned only through the Spirit." It is the Holy Spirit who reveals the Word to us.

> But when he, the Spirit of truth, comes, he will guide you into all the truth. He will not speak on his own; he will speak only what he hears, and he will tell you what is yet to come. (John 16:13)

The Holy Spirit speaks to us, and the Holy Spirit "speaks only what he hears" from God. Therefore, the Word is alive because it is God talking to the Holy Spirit and the Holy Spirit interprets God's words for our understanding. When you read the Word, know your understanding is from the voice of God.

> We know that we have come to know him if we keep his commands. (1 John 2:3)

The Holy Spirit opens our heart to the Word as Christ leads us in our ministry. Our walk with the Lord depends on knowing the Word, and our walk opens our heart to hear the Spirit, which gives us a deeper understanding of the Word. The Word becomes alive and active because God speaks to us through the Spirit as we read the Scripture. The more we are in the Word, the more we recognize the Spirit and the more alive the Word becomes. This brings us closer to God, with a better understanding of him and his perfect love for us. The more of Christ's love we give, the more we understand Christ and the more love our heart can receive.

> The Spirit gives life; the flesh counts for nothing. The words I have spoken to you—they are full of the Spirit and life. (John 6:63)

Christ said his words are life and spirit. The Holy Spirit gives us discernment of the Word and life to our soul. The flesh counts for nothing in giving life to our soul.

In this life, we try to satisfy our eternal soul through the flesh by seeking temporal things. Our flesh is temporal; therefore, it seeks temporal worldly things. Our soul is eternal; therefore, it seeks eternal things. The only thing that permanently satisfies our eternal soul is the eternal Spirit. When your soul is satisfied by the Spirit, it will stop searching for satisfaction through the flesh, and then you can truly enjoy the world the way God meant for you to enjoy the world.

> The thief comes only to steal and kill and destroy; I have come that they may have life, and have it to the full. (John 10:10)

Explain how God's Word is alive.

_____

_____

_____

Explain what Christ means by "the flesh counts for nothing" in John 6:63.

_____

_____

_____

Living by the Word

Below are five ways the Word is needed in our everyday walk, serving the Lord.

1. The Word is needed for spiritual warfare because we need the power of the Word to fight off Satan's temptations, just as Christ did after his forty day fast in the desert (Matthew 4:1–11).

Take the helmet of salvation and the sword of the Spirit, which is the word of God. (Ephesians 6:17)

2. We need knowledge of the Word so we can teach about God's love and encourage others by sharing his divine plan to save us through Christ. Without understanding the Word and knowing the Scriptures, it is virtually impossible to minister to others.

   All Scripture is God-breathed and is useful for teaching, rebuking, correcting and training in righteousness. (2 Timothy 3:16)

3. Faith comes from hearing the Word which reveals God's love. We cannot develop a relationship with the Lord without his Word. We read the Bible to understand his ways and to personally know him by walking in obedience to his Word. The closer we are to the Lord, the more we know his love and the more we will trust him.

   Consequently, faith comes from hearing the message, and the message is heard through the word about Christ. (Romans 10:17)

   We know that we have come to know him if we keep his commands. (1 John 2:3)

4. We cannot walk with the Lord without understanding his commands and promises. Our walk is centered on God's love, and without the Word, we cannot understand his perfect love for us. The Word is alive, and God speaks to us through his Word. The more we are in the Word, the more we can recognize the Spirit.

   Jesus answered, "It is written: 'Man shall not live on bread alone, but on every word that comes from the mouth of God.'" (Matthew 4:4)

   Your word is a lamp to my feet, a light on my path. (Psalm 119:105)

5. The Word offers us comfort as we read about God's love and his promise to always be with us. As we read the psalms, we can understand David's emotional states and how he went to the Lord for comfort.

   Praise be to the God and Father of our Lord Jesus Christ, the Father of compassion and the God of all comfort, who comforts us in all our troubles, so that we can comfort those in any trouble with the comfort we ourselves receive from God. (2 Corinthians 1:3–4)

John said, "We come to know him if we keep his commands." How does this help us understand the Word?

_____

_____

_____

How does comforting others benefit us?

_____

_____

_____

Summary

The Bible is the divine voice of God, revealing his love for us and his divine guidance for us. The Bible was inspired by God, and we can believe every word is true. Therefore, we can believe all of God's promises.

> And we also thank God continually because, when you received the word of God, which you heard from us, you accepted it not as a human word, but as it actually is, the word of God, which is indeed at work in you who believe. (1 Thessalonians 2:13)

I have personally found that the more I minister to others, the more I need to be in the Word. The more we serve the Lord, the closer we are to him and the more we will seek him through his Word. The Word is alive, and when Christ is our life, the Word becomes more alive. You can read the Word every day for the rest of your life and God will reveal new insight because he always has more to say. Reading the Word can become conversation with God if we pray before and during reading the Word. Read the Word, and realize that God is speaking to you and be comforted as the Word pulls you into the Spirit. Let it fill you with peace and joy.

Lesson 8: The Gift of Faith

Introduction

Without faith it is impossible to please God (Hebrews 11:6), and without faith it is impossible to walk with God. The Bible has much to say about faith, and God identifies people in the Bible with whom he credits with having faith. We will look at Abraham's faith and how God tested the faith of the Israelites and how he tests our faith. Living in a world of tragedies, we may question God or complain to God, making it difficult to maintain our faith. We will look at both our viewpoint and God's concerning tragedies in life that test our faith. In this lesson, we will see how faith is essential in our walk, how we obtain faith, why God wants us to have faith, and how our faith can grow stronger.

The following are the words from a tearful prayer by Billy Graham: "I was trying to be on the level with God, but something remained unspoken. At last the Holy Spirit freed me to say it. 'Father, I am going to accept this as Thy Word—by *faith!* I'm going to allow faith to go beyond my intellectual questions and doubts, and I will believe this to be Your inspired Word."[18] As we walk with the Lord with an open mind and an open heart, we will learn through the Holy Spirit to trust him completely because he is sovereign and his love for us endures forever.

Faith and Trust

> Now faith is confidence in what we hope for and assurance about what we do not see. (Hebrews 11:1)

> Trust in the LORD with all your heart and lean not on your own understanding. (Proverbs 3:5)

Faith is a knowing in our heart, and trust is putting our faith into action. For example, faith tells me I can parachute out of an airplane and land safely; trust occurs when I jump. Our faith in the Lord is shown by our willingness to trust him, and we do that by surrendering our will to his will. Do you trust the Lord to lead your life?

Then Jesus said to his disciples, "Whoever wants to be my disciple must deny themselves and take up their cross and follow me." (Matthew 16:24)

When we follow Christ even when we don't feel like it, don't understand, or are fearful, we are trusting in him. We trust the Lord's directions because he is Lord, and we trust his will over our will. This is obedience.

And without faith it is impossible to please God, because anyone who comes to him must believe that he exists and that he rewards those who earnestly seek him. (Hebrews 11:6)

Looking at this verse from another perspective, we can say that there is nothing that pleases God more than for us to trust him. Our love for the Lord is revealed through our trusting him.

Why do you think it is impossible to please God without faith?

_____

_____

_____

Describe what it would be like to have perfect faith in the Lord.

_____

_____

_____

Faith and Obedience

If you love me, keep my commands. (John 14:15)

The Lord delights in obedience because it shows our faith.

But Samuel replied: "Does the Lord delight in burnt offerings and sacrifices as much as in obeying the Lord? To obey is better than sacrifice, and to heed is better than the fat of rams." (1 Samuel 15:22)

Samuel was telling King Saul that the Lord delights in obedience more than in the act of formal worship (burnt offerings). This means we can go to Sunday worship and praise God all day, but without faithful obedience throughout the week, we cannot please God.

Abraham believed God, and it was credited to him as righteousness. (Romans 4:3)

Abraham showed his faith when God told him to sacrifice his only son. We know from the story in Genesis that God stopped the sacrifice at the last minute and supplied a lamb, but this command revealed Abraham's heart, his love and fear of the Lord. Although Abraham was not perfect in his decisions, when he had a direct command from the Lord, he obeyed.

> When they reached the place God had told him about, Abraham built an altar there and arranged the wood on it. He bound his son Isaac and laid him on the altar, on top of the wood. Then he reached out his hand and took the knife to slay his son. But the angel of the LORD called out to him from heaven, "Abraham! Abraham!" "Here I am," he replied. "Do not lay a hand on the boy," he said. "Do not do anything to him. Now I know that you fear God, because you have not withheld from me your son, your only son." (Genesis 22:9–12)

Abraham believed God, and it was credited to him as righteousness. Abraham was blessed and his name is great, just as God promised. God was pleased with Abraham's faith as demonstrated by his obedience. God is just as pleased when we show our faith by obedience, especially when obedience may be difficult and require sacrifice on our part.

> What does Scripture say? "Abraham believed God, and it was credited to him as righteousness." (Romans 4:3)

Abraham was the father of the Israelite nation, the nation God chose to be his people, and through this nation other nations would see the true God. The Israelites' faith wavered as they crossed the desert on their way to the Promised Land. They were slaves in Egypt, and God chose Moses as their leader. God caused ten miraculous plaques to fall upon the Egyptians, including the death of firstborn male children and animals of the Egyptians. This prompted Pharaoh to finally release the Israelites from their slavery. God lead the Israelites across the desert with a pillar of cloud during the day and a pillar of fire in the evening.

Many times the Israelites lost their faith in the journey across the desert. When they finally arrived at the land God had promised them, most of the spies who went into the Promised Land came back with a fearful report.

> But the men… said, "We can't attack those people; they are stronger than we are." And they spread among the Israelites a bad report about the land they had explored. They said, "The land we explored devours those living in it. All the people we saw there are of great size. We saw the Nephilim there (the descendants of Anak come from the Nephilim). We seemed like grasshoppers in our own eyes, and we looked the same to them." (Numbers 13:31–33)

Because of their unbelief, God refused to let that generation into the Promised Land, causing them to spend forty years in the desert. The people did not believe God's promises or his divine power. The Israelites saw no solution based on their own power, so they limited their expectation of God's power. God was not pleased with the Israelites and their continuing lack of faith.

God is pleased and blesses those who trust him, but he is hurt and angry when we do not trust him. Imagine how great the life of the Israelites would have been if they had trusted God. Trust the Lord because all things are possible for God, and he loves you perfectly. Don't spend forty years in the desert.

Whenever people of God are overcome by fear or grief due to trials and tribulations of this life, there is a temptation to seek refuge or guidance separate from God. But this is the time to run to God with all your emotions and troubles and beg for his help, strength, comfort, and guidance. In our most desperate moments, we need to reach our heart out to God and to God's people. The Lord knows our pain and suffering, and he has both hands stretched out to comfort and guide us in his perfect love. This is a time to carefully follow the Lord in obedience as he leads us through the difficult times in life.

> Jesus looked at them and said, "With man this is impossible; but with God all things are possible." (Matthew 19:26)

There is nothing in our lives that is impossible for God. Remember this truth when you pray. Sometimes situations in life seem impossible for us and we forget that all things are possible for God. God can change our situation and sometimes he does, but he promises that he will always give us the strength, wisdom, patience, and his divine power to overcome anything this world puts in our path, if we walk in his will.

Why do you think God desires obedience over sacrifice (1 Samuel 15:22)?

_____

_____

_____

How is our love for God revealed by our obedience (John 14:15)?

_____

_____

_____

Growing in Faith

How do we obtain faith, and do we gain more faith the longer we walk with the Lord? The longer we know someone and we become closer friends, the more we can trust them. The same is true with God. Our faith grows as we develop a closer relationship with the Lord. We do this by studying his Word and serving him. Studying the Word and serving the Lord go together. The more we serve the Lord by ministering to people, the more we need knowledge of his Word. When we are both in the Word and serving the Lord, we continually grow closer to the Lord, thereby increasing our faith in him. Our faith will reach a point where our will is to always seek God's will.

> Consequently, faith comes from hearing the message, and the message is heard through the word about Christ. (Romans 10:17)

> We know that we have come to know him if we keep his commands. (1 John 2:3)

Through reading his Word and walking in obedience to the Lord, we come to know him, developing a close, personal relationship that leads to more faith. Faith leads us to more peace and more security in Christ, which can motivate us to know the Lord more. Faith is necessary to follow the Spirit, and faith is necessary to have peace and security in Christ.

A powerful story for understanding faith is given in the story of Job, who feared God and shunned evil.

> In the land of Uz there lived a man whose name was Job. This man was blameless and upright; he feared God and shunned evil. (Job 1:1)

Job was very prosperous when he suddenly lost his ten children, servants, camels, and sheep (Job 1). Then he became sick and was covered with sores from his feet to crown of his head (Job 2:7). His three friends tried to console him by attempting to explain the reason for his tragedies. They assumed it was due to Job's sins, but Job denied any sins that would cause his tragedy. Job remained faithful to God throughout his tragedies, even though he wanted to know why all these tragedies had happened.

> I cry out to you, O God, but you do not answer; I stand up, but you merely look at me. You turn on me ruthlessly; with the might of your hand you attack me. (Job 30:20–21)

Then the Lord spoke to Job out of the storm. He said: "Who is this that obscures my plans with words without knowledge? (Job 38:1–2). God explained to Job that he was God. He asked Job if he could do the things that only God can do, revealing that Job could not possibly understand all the ways of God. God never addressed Job's tragedies but was pleased with Job's faith and called him his servant.

> The Lord blessed the latter part of Job's life more than the first. (Job 42:12)

God's ways and thoughts are above ours, just as the heavens are higher than the earth (Isaiah 55:9). Let your faith in God be stronger than whatever happens in this world, stronger than your understanding, and know God is in control and will soon make all things right. God doesn't promise an explanation for what happens to us in this life, but he does promise that if we trust him, he will carry us through to our eternal home with him. Pray about everything, and accept God's divine will and plan. Always trust, praise, and thank God, no matter what life brings to you.

> To the one who is victorious, I will give the right to sit with me on my throne, just as I was victorious and sat down with my Father on his throne. (Revelation 3:21)

Explain how we can gain more faith.

_____

_____

_____

Describe the faith that God wants us to have.

_____

_____

_____

Summary

How can we possibly walk with the Lord and have any peace if do not have faith? It is a powerful statement that God makes when he says it is impossible to please him if we do not have faith. We can see from the stories of Abraham and Job how pleased God is when we show faith and from the story of the Israelites how displeased God is when we lack faith. When we trust the Lord, it tells him that we know him and love him and that we know his perfect love for us and his ways are always perfect. Trust in the Lord means we trust his ways over our ways, our feelings, and our understanding. Remember, his ways and thoughts are higher than our ways and thoughts, as the heavens are higher than the earth (Isaiah 55:8–9). We are always blessed when we trust the Lord and obey his good, pleasing, and perfect will. Know that Lord will always guide you in the right direction, toward eternity with him, because he loves you more than words can say. Trust the Lord because he is Lord.

Lesson 9: God Is with Us

Introduction

"And surely I am with you always, to the very end of the age" (Matthew 28:20). These are the words Christ spoke just before he ascended to the Father. In this lesson, we will see that Scripture reveals God's love for us and his desire to always be with us. Once we realize the continuous presence of the Lord through the Holy Spirit, it can give us a feeling of security and an awareness of belonging to God's family. Christ said, "For indeed, the kingdom of God is within you" (Luke 17:21 NKJV), and that is where we live, in God's eternal kingdom.

God fills us with the Holy Spirit, enabling us to have a close, loving relationship with him. God desires for us to know him and walk closely with him every day, and we can have a relationship with the Lord, through the Spirit, that is closer and more intimate than any other relationship in life. God desires to always be with us, and the depth of our relationship depends on how close we want to be to him. "You will seek me and will find me when you seek me with all your heart" (Jeremiah 29:13).

God's Presence with Us

God's original intent was to walk with Adam and Eve in the garden forever, to always be in their presence and have a close relationship with them. God's desire is always to be with us and for us always to want to be in his presence.

> Then the man and his wife heard the sound of the LORD God as he was walking in the garden in the cool of the day. (Genesis 3:8)

God revealed his presence to the Israelite people. He led them through the desert by a pillar of fire at night and a pillar of cloud by day, showing the people that he was with them.

> By day the LORD went ahead of them in a pillar of cloud to guide them on their way and by night in a pillar of fire to give them light, so that they could travel by day or night. (Exodus 13:21)

God also was with the Israelites in the tent of meeting.

> Now Moses used to take a tent and pitch it outside the camp some distance away, calling it the "tent of meeting." Anyone inquiring of the LORD would go to the tent of meeting outside the camp. And whenever Moses went out to the tent, all the people rose and stood at the entrances to their tents, watching Moses until he entered the tent. As Moses went into the tent, the pillar of cloud would come down and stay at the entrance, while the LORD spoke with Moses. (Exodus 33:7–9)

The term *tent of meeting* is used in Exodus, Leviticus, and Numbers, and later, the term *tabernacle of Moses* is used. The tabernacle was constructed in accordance with God's directions and housed the ark of the covenant, which contained the Ten Commandments. The tabernacle was considered God's house and was to be carried with the Israelites as they wandered the desert.

King Solomon built the first temple as a place to worship God and experience his presence.

> And it came to pass, when the priests came out of the holy place, that the cloud filled the house of the LORD, so that the priests could not continue ministering because of the cloud; for the glory of the LORD filled the house of the LORD. Then Solomon spoke: "The LORD said He would dwell in the dark cloud. I have surely built You an exalted house, and a place for You to dwell in forever." (1 Kings 8:10–13 NKJV)

When Solomon dedicated the temple, God made his presence shown by filling the temple with a cloud. God wanted the Israelites to know he was with them.

> "Am I only a God nearby," declares the LORD, "and not a God far away? Who can hide in secret places so that I cannot see him?" declares the LORD. "Do I not fill heavens and earth?" declares the LORD. (Jeremiah 23:23–24)

A powerful story that clearly illustrates that God is with his people is the story about Gideon. The Israelites were trying to escape from the power of Midian by preparing shelters for themselves in mountain clefts, caves, and strongholds.

> The angel of the LORD came and sat down under the oak in Ophrah that belonged to Joash the Abiezrite, where his son Gideon was threshing wheat in a winepress to keep it from the Midianites. When the angel of the LORD appeared to Gideon, he said, "The LORD is with you, mighty warrior." ....The LORD turned to him and said, "Go in the strength you have and save Israel out of Midian's hand. Am I not sending you?"Pardon me, my lord," Gideon replied,

"but how can I save Israel? My clan is the weakest in Manasseh, and I am the least in my family." (Judges 6:11–12, 14-15)

This was a monumental task for Gideon, far above his capabilities as the weakest in his clan. Why do you think God called him "mighty warrior"? Does God ever call you to do something that you believe is above your capability? Remember God said to Gideon, "The Lord is with you," and he will be with you too.

> The Lord answered, "I will be with you, and you will strike down all the Midianites, leaving none alive." (Judges 6:16)

> Early in the morning, Jerub-Baal (that is, Gideon) and all his men camped at the spring of Harod. The camp of Midian was north of them in the valley near the hill of Moreh. The Lord said to Gideon, "You have too many men. I cannot deliver Midian into their hands, or Israel would boast against me, 'My own strength has saved me.' Now announce to the army, 'Anyone who trembles with fear may turn back and leave Mount Gilead.' " So twenty-two thousand men left, while ten thousand remained.

> But the Lord said to Gideon, "There are still too many men. Take them down to the water, and I will thin them out for you there. If I say, 'This one shall go with you,' he shall go; but if I say, 'This one shall not go with you,' he shall not go."

> So Gideon took the men down to the water. There the Lord told him, "Separate those who lap the water with their tongues as a dog laps from those who kneel down to drink." Three hundred of them drank from cupped hands, lapping like dogs. All the rest got down on their knees to drink.

> The Lord said to Gideon, "With the three hundred men that lapped I will save you and give the Midianites into your hands. Let all the others go home." So Gideon sent the rest of the Israelites home but kept the three hundred, who took over the provisions and trumpets of the others. (Judges 7:1–8)

God gave the Israelites victory because Gideon obeyed God. Victory even with what we would consider impossible odds because all things are possible with God. Know God is with you; follow him in obedience and you will also be victorious according to God's plan.

Describe what it means to know God is always with you and loves you perfectly.

_____

_____

_____

The apostle Paul stated, "For when I am weak, then I am strong" (2 Corinthians 12:10). How does this verse relate with the story of Gideon, and how can it relate to knowing God is with us?

_____

_____

_____

God's Presence in Us

The Lord is always with us, and his desire is for us to be aware of his presence. He walked in the garden with Adam and made his presence revealed in the tabernacle and in the temple. But God desires to be even closer to his people, so Christ came to earth.

One of the names for God is Immanuel, which means "God with us." Christ appeared as a man, humbled himself, and died a sacrificial death on the cross for our sins to redeem us to God. After three days he arose, and his last words before descending to the Father were, "And surely I am with you always, to the very end of the age" (Matthew 28:20).

The Lord promises to be with us always, and he does this by living in us through the Holy Spirit.

> If you love me, keep my commands. And I will ask the Father, and he will give you another advocate to help you and be with you forever—the Spirit of truth. The world cannot accept him, because it neither sees him nor knows him. But you know him, for he lives with you and will be in you. (John 14:15–17)

The Lord is always with us, every second of every day for all eternity, as he lives in us. As we learn to live in the Spirit, communing with God, thanking and praising him, reading his Word, fellowshipping with other believers, and serving him, we will become more aware of the Holy Spirit as he changes our heart. Just as God showed his presence by filling the temple with a cloud, he will show his presence by filling us with the Holy Spirit. We are the temple.

God is with us, and we need to be with God. We can train ourselves to be attentive, seeing God in all things. "This is the clarifying light that I seek: to be 'clear at center' and so with true attentiveness 'to see God in all things, and all things in God,'" said Leighton Ford in his book *The Attentive Life*.[19]

> Come near to God and he will come near to you. (James 4:8)

> Jesus replied, "Anyone who loves me will obey my teaching. My Father will love them, and we will come to them and make our home with them." (John 14:23)

The story of Steven's stoning reveals the powerful presence of the Father and the Son. Some of the Jews from the synagogue called "Freedmen" began to argue with Steven and persuaded some men to lie and say Steven spoke words of blasphemy. Steven was taken before the high priest and Sanhedrin to face the charges by the false witnesses. Steven told them the history of the Israelite people from Abraham up to the time when the Jews crucified Christ. He called them "stiffed-neck people" and "uncircumcised heart." The response of the Sanhedrin was not favorable.

> When the members of the Sanhedrin heard this, they were furious and gnashed their teeth at him. But Stephen, full of the Holy Spirit, looked up to heaven and saw the glory of God, and Jesus standing at the right hand of God. "Look," he said, "I see heaven open and the Son of Man standing at the right hand of God." At this they covered their ears and, yelling at the top of their voices, they all rushed at him, dragged him out of the city and began to stone him. (Acts 7:54–58)

Heaven opened, and Steven saw Christ standing at the right hand of God. The Father and the Son were definitely with Steven every step and showed themselves at just the right time. Can you imagine the strength Steven received when heaven opened and he saw the Father and the Son waiting for him? Heaven may not open for you and me, but the Father and Son are with us every step, just as they were with Steven.

Another story that shows that God is always with us is the story of Paul during the shipwreck. Paul was en route to Rome to stand trial before Caesar when a violent storm came up that threatened to sink the ship. The crew finally gave up all hope of being saved.

> But now I urge you to keep up your courage, because not one of you will be lost; only the ship will be destroyed. Last night an angel of the God to whom I belong and whom I serve stood beside me and said, "Do not be afraid, Paul. You must stand trial before Caesar; and God has graciously given you the lives of all who sail with you." So keep up your courage, men, for I have faith in God that it will happen just as he told me. (Acts 27:22–25)

God sent an angel to comfort Paul and to inform him what was going to happen and what he needed to do. God was with Paul and sent help when Paul needed it. Notice Paul told the men about the angel and God's directions to save the crew, thereby giving God the glory.

When we are in difficult circumstances, know God is with you and will guide you through. He may not send an angel, but he will speak to you through prayer, his Word, or godly counsel. This is a promise of God.

So do not fear, for I am with you; do not be dismayed, for I am your God. I will strengthen you and help you; I will uphold you with my righteous right hand. (Isaiah 41:10)

The Holy Spirit lives in us, and Christ intercedes on our behalf to the Father. We are never alone; God (Father, Son, and Holy Spirit) is always with us. God always desires for us to seek him and know him so he can be closer to us and bless us forever.

How did it help Steven when heaven opened and he saw the Christ standing at the right hand of God?

_____

_____

_____

What gave Paul the courage he needed as the ship was about to be destroyed?

_____

_____

_____

Summary

God's desire to be with you is clearly seen all throughout the Bible. God revealed his presence walking with Adam in the garden, in the pillar of cloud and the pillar of fire, in the tabernacle, and in the temple. God reveals himself to us through the Holy Spirit, with the Father and Son making their home with us, (John 14:33). This tells us how much God loves us and desires to be with us forever.

Know the love that God has for you and that he is always with you. Let this truth always reside in your heart, and continue to receive God's love by reflecting his love to others. The greatest thing in life is to know that God is always with you and his love fills your heart.

Lesson 10: The Mind of Christ

Introduction

As we discussed earlier, God has created us with the ability to renew our mind, wiring in new memories and unwiring old toxic memories. Dr. Caroline Leaf, in her book *Switch on Your Brain*, explains,

> The scientific power of our mind to change the brain is called *epigenetics* and spiritually it is as a man thinks so is he (Prov. 23:7). The way the brain changes as a result of mental activity is scientifically called *neuroplasticity*, and spiritually, it is the renewing of the mind (Rom. 12:2.).[20] Science and Scripture both show that we are wired for love and optimism.[21] Toxic thinking will change your brain wiring in a negative direction and throw your mind and body into stress, which affects our body's natural healing capacities… Research shows that 75 to 98 percent of mental, physical, and behavioral illness comes from one's thought life … Taking this to a deeper level, research shows that DNA actually changes shape according to our thoughts … Studies have shown that thinking and feeling anger, fear, unforgiveness, and frustration caused DNA to change shape according to thoughts and feelings.[22]

Old toxic thoughts can be removed from our brains and new godly thoughts wired into our brains. The longer we walk with the Lord, the more our old sinful patterns of life diminish, having less real estate in our brains. What a blessing it is to be our own brain surgeons and change our thinking, to control our thinking, and to receive God's peace and joy. God and his perfect love for us have saved us through Christ, filled us with the Holy Spirit, given us a new identity, and made us part of his eternal family, and created us so he can change us to have the mind of Christ.

> We have the mind of Christ. (1 Corinthians 2:16)

We are created in the image of God, and our mind can be renewed to be like the mind of Christ. After all, *Christian* means "Christlike." From Scripture, let us see the mind of Christ and how our mind is renewed.

The Mind of Love

> For the Son of Man came to seek and to save the lost. (Luke 19:10)

> When he saw the crowds, he had compassion on them, because they were harassed and helpless, like sheep without a shepherd. (Matthew 9:36)

> And being found in appearance as a man, he humbled himself by becoming obedient to death—even death on a cross! (Philippians 2:8)

> Just as the Son of Man did not come to be served, but to serve, and to give his life as a ransom for many. (Matthew 20:28)

First John 4:8 states, "God is love." Jesus has a heart of love and compassion. He was humble and came to serve and to save the lost, to save all mankind through his sacrifice on the cross. Christ revealed his love by performing many miracles for others, but he performed none for himself.

God is continually molding us to have the mind of Christ, a mind of love and compassion with a serving heart. The mind of Christ is present in the indwelling Holy Spirit.

> But the fruit of the Spirit is love, joy, peace, patience, kindness, goodness, faithfulness, gentleness and self-control. (Galatians 5:22–23)

> Love is patient, love is kind. It does not envy, it does not boast, it is not proud. It does not dishonor others, it is not self-seeking, it is not easily angered, it keeps no record of wrongs. Love does not delight in evil but rejoices with the truth. It always protects, always trusts, always hopes, always perseveres. Love never fails. (1 Corinthians 13:4–8)

God desires that we go through this life with peace and joy and with a mind of love and hope. Love is the greatest commandment and the foundation of our Christian life.

> "Teacher, which is the greatest commandment in the Law?" Jesus replied: "'Love the Lord your God with all your heart and with all your soul and with all your mind.' This is the first and greatest commandment. And the second is like it: 'Love your neighbor as yourself.'" (Matthew 22:36–40)

A mind of love is a mind that trusts God and overcomes fear. Fear is Satan's number-one weapon, and a mind of fear can lead to a mind of worry, anxiety, anger, unforgiveness, and impatience. As our mind is continually being renewed, we develop more love and trust in the Lord, which replaces fear.

There is no fear in love. But perfect love drives out fear. (1 John 4:18)

The more love we have for God and others, the more secure we are in Christ and the less fear we have. Whenever Satan attacks us with fear, we immediately give it to the Lord and ask for peace. We put our worry and fear into his hands and ask him to guide us through the day with godly wisdom, strength, and his divine power to get through whatever it is we fear. Whenever fear attacks, run to God. Where did Christ go when he was in the garden and was tempted and tested with fear? He bowed to the ground and went to the Father in prayer, and the Father sent an angel to comfort and strengthen him.

> Do not be anxious about anything, but in every situation, by prayer and petition, with thanksgiving, present your requests to God. And the peace of God, which transcends all understanding, will guard your hearts and your minds in Christ Jesus. (Philippians 4:6–7)

A mind of Christ knows of God's perfect love and that the Father and the Son are always with us.

> For I am convinced that neither death nor life, neither angels nor demons, neither the present nor the future, nor any powers, neither height nor depth, nor anything else in all creation, will be able to separate us from the love of God that is in Christ Jesus our Lord. (Romans 8:38–39)

Explain how God's perfect love can cast out our fears.

_____

_____

_____

Describe what it would be like to have the mind of Christ.

_____

_____

_____

Renewing the Mind

> Do not conform to the pattern of this world, but be transformed by the renewing of your mind. (Romans 12:2)

The key to renewing the mind is being aware of what we are thinking and controlling our thoughts and emotions.

We demolish arguments and every pretension that sets itself up against the knowledge of God, and we take captive every thought to make it obedient to Christ. (2 Corinthians 10:5)

We control our thoughts by first capturing them. This gives us time to replace our thoughts with godly wisdom. The longer we entertain the sinful or negative thought, the more difficult it will be to gain control of that thought. If our thoughts and behaviors are controlled by our emotions, we have become slaves to our feelings. If we handle the events occurring each day with godly wisdom, our mind will be renewed. Dr. Leaf writes,

> When we distort love and truth, we wire this perversion into our brains and, in a sense create brain damage. This is not an exaggeration, because our brains are wired for love, not fear, and therefore all the circuits—neurochemical, neural physiological, neurobiological, and electromagnetic—are geared up for healthy, not toxic thinking. If we allow ourselves to learn fear, it creates chaos and havoc in our brains.[23]

Dr. Jennings states,

> When people exercise their will to choose to act in a manner that violates reason and conscience, they damage themselves, becoming restless, uneasy, and anxious. But when the will follows the direction of reason and conscience, then even though it might not feel good at the time, healing occurs, and internal peace, confidence, and contentment result.[24]

When we use reason and conscience to make Godly decisions, it gives us the strength to overcome toxic thoughts and helps us to gain control over our emotions.

The brain's neural circuits rewire according to how we think. Consider the following analogy: Picture a path through the woods. The more we walk on the path, the wider the path gets, making it easier to walk. The more we think about something, the more neural connections are made, making it easier to access the thought. What happens when we stop walking on the wooded path? Weeds grow over, making it difficult for walking. When we stop thinking the toxic thought, the associated neural connections in our brain, like the well-worn path, begin breaking down, making it more difficult to access the toxic thoughts. Just as it takes time for the weeds to grow over the trail, it takes time for the brain's neural circuits to breakdown. The longer we stop walking on the path, the more overgrown it becomes. We do this by replacing toxic thoughts with godly thoughts, thus creating new clear paths.

> Finally, brothers and sisters, whatever is true, whatever is noble, whatever is right, whatever is pure, whatever is lovely, whatever is admirable—if anything is excellent and praiseworthy—think about such things. (Philippians 4:8)

Meditating on God's love makes positive changes in our brain.

> Dr. Newberg at the University of Pennsylvania has documented that all forms of contemplative meditation were associated with positive brain changes—but the greatest improvements occurred when participants meditated specifically on a God of love. Such meditation was associated with growth in the prefrontal cortex (the part of the brain right behind the forehead where we reason, make judgments and experience Godlike love) and subsequent increased capacity for empathy, sympathy, compassion and altruism. But here's the most astonishing part. Not only does other-centered love increase when we worship a God of love, but sharp thinking and memory improve as well. In other words, worshiping a God of love actually stimulates the brain to heal and grow.[25]

> But whose delight is in the law of the LORD, and who meditates on his law day and night. (Psalm 1:2)

We overcome evil by doing good. We cannot think the toxic thoughts away; we have to change toxic thoughts to new thoughts. The key is to replace old habits and old thoughts with new habits and new thoughts because this is how the brain will renew. Activities like Bible reading, praying, ministering to others, Bible studies, church assemblies, and church activities will help renew the mind, replacing old activities with godly activities.

> Do not be overcome by evil, but overcome evil with good. (Romans 12:21)

Knowing that the neurons in our brain connect and disconnect by the way we think gives us the insight to control our thoughts because we become aware that we are rewiring our brain. This takes patience and persistence because the brain rewires slowly. If we continue to capture our toxic thoughts of fear, anger, resentments, lust, etc. with thoughts of peace, hope, love, success, etc., our brain will rewire. To speed up this rewiring process, each day take time to meditate on Scriptures that reveal God's love. Write them down, take them with you, and read them often.

Essential to renewing the mind is to replace a toxic thought with a godly thought. This can be difficult when comes to our emotions. Satan normally attacks us through our emotions, such as irrational fear, anger, lust, greed, etc. Often these emotions appear to be automatic reactions to the situation; we may say or do something quickly that we later regret. I personally had a difficult time in overcoming my anger because it started when I was about seven years of age. At the age of fifty nine, my anger was still with me. For example, if I couldn't find the hammer in the garage, I would often explode into a rage, throwing, kicking, and breaking things. When I surrendered my heart to Christ, I prayed that he would help destroy this anger that was in me. For the next two years, I prayed, read Christian books on anger, and took video courses on overcoming anger. The verse that had a great impact on my recovery is James 1:19: "My dear brothers and sisters, take note of this: Everyone should be quick to listen, slow to speak and slow to become angry."

Whenever my anger ignited, I would keep my mouth shut, which tended to keep me physically in control. It was difficult and I often failed, but I prayed and never gave up. Now twelve years later, I find myself rarely getting angry. If Satan attacks me with anger, I remain still in Christ, take that anger to godly wisdom, and reap the glory of victory. Satan no longer steals my peace and joy with anger. When we take our toxic emotions to God in prayer, we overcome fear and ask the Lord for the peace that transcends understanding.

Describe the process of how the mind renews.

_____

_____

_____

Explain the advantages of exercising James 1:19. "My dear brothers and sisters, take note of this: Everyone should be quick to listen, slow to speak and slow to become angry."

_____

_____

_____

Summary

When we seriously think about what it means to have the mind of Christ, it reveals the unbelievable love God has for us. He has created us so that our minds can be renewed and rewired, erasing toxic thoughts and desires and replacing them with godly thoughts. This was a miracle for me because I had fifty-nine years of toxic thoughts and uncontrollable emotions that he replaced with thoughts of love, peace, and joy. What a blessing God has for you by molding you to have the mind of Christ. It is God's priority to make us like Christ. The more Christ-minded we become, the more we understand God and his Word, the more we trust him, and the more we will seek to serve him and walk according to his perfect will for us.

When we understand that God is molding us to have the mind of Christ, it can give us a better understanding of how God is guiding us through life. We can see how we are changing as a result of whatever we are going through. So let every situation mold you to have the mind of Christ, a mind of love, peace, joy, and godly wisdom. However, know that it takes time for the brain to rewire, so exercise patience, persistence, and faith. Celebrate with every little victory that brings you closer to the mind of Christ.

Lesson 11: God Is Faithful

Introduction

Understanding God's faithfulness is essential if we want to walk with the Lord, putting our trust in him. If God were not perfectly faithful, how could we believe in his promises? Our faith comes from hearing the Word of God and learning about his faithfulness as he fulfilled the promises he made to Abraham, the Israelites, David, and many others. God's promises are also revealed through the many prophecies, including the prophecies of Christ.

This week we will look at examples of God's faithfulness and how believing God's promises gives us faith and security. Sometimes God's promises are not revealed to us in a way we were expecting, and this can cause us to doubt. We will see that God's ways are not always our ways, but God's ways are always perfect and good.

> "For my thoughts are not your thoughts, neither are your ways my ways," declares the LORD. "As the heavens are higher than the earth, so are my ways higher than your ways and my thoughts than your thoughts." (Isaiah 55:8–9)

God's Promises

God made a promise to Abraham and Sarah, saying they would have a son in their old age. Sometimes we view God's promises as impossible, but God can do things through us that we cannot do for ourselves.

> God also said to Abraham, "As for Sarai your wife, you are no longer to call her Sarai; her name will be Sarah. I will bless her and will surely give you a son by her. I will bless her so that she will be the mother of nations; kings of peoples will come from her." Abraham fell facedown; he laughed and said to himself, "Will a son be born to a man a hundred years old? Will Sarah bear a child at the age of ninety?" (Genesis 17:15–17)

When things are beyond our understanding and capabilities, remember "all things are possible for God" (Matthew 19:26). Just as God performed a miracle for Abraham and Sarah, he will perform miracles for you if you trust in his faithfulness.

> Now the LORD was gracious to Sarah as he had said, and the LORD did for Sarah what he had promised. Sarah became pregnant and bore a son to Abraham in his old age, at the very time God had promised him. (Genesis 21:1–2)

Abraham and Sarah waited twenty-five years before their son, Isaac, was born. When you pray requesting God's promises, remember all things are possible for God and wait patiently. Patience is required when waiting on God's promise because God's ways are not our ways and his timing is not our timing. God's priority is to mold us to be like Christ and guide us in his divine plan for our lives. God wants us to trust him totally, leaving everything in his control, continually praying as he guides us through the Holy Spirit as we live for Christ. If we pray and expect God's faithfulness to occur on our schedule and the way we desire, we will soon lose our faith. True faith in God's promises is leaving everything in his hands.

David trusted God's faithfulness when he killed Goliath and continued to trust God throughout his life. He trusted God during the years he was running from Saul and exhibited patience waiting on the Lord. David never lost a battle because he trusted God and asked for his guidance.

> Now when the Philistines heard that they had anointed David king over Israel, all the Philistines went up to search for David. And David heard of it and went down to the stronghold. The Philistines also went and deployed themselves in the Valley of Rephaim. So David inquired of the LORD, saying, "Shall I go up against the Philistines? Will You deliver them into my hand?"
>
> And the LORD said to David, "Go up, for I will doubtless deliver the Philistines into your hand."
>
> So David went to Baal Perazim, and David defeated them there; and he said, "The LORD has broken through my enemies before me, like a breakthrough of water." Therefore he called the name of that place Baal Perazim. (2 Samuel 5:17–20 NKJV)

David inquired of the Lord before he went into battle, asking the Lord for his guidance. David and his army fought the Philistines, giving their best to God, knowing they would be victorious no matter what the odds. When David defeated the Philistines, he praised God, giving God the glory for the victory. Like David, we can ask God for guidance in making our decisions, and when we are victorious, all the glory goes to God. God will join us in our battles just as he joined David in his battles.

The history of Israel is a story of a nation that sometimes walked with God and sometimes walked away from God and worshipped false gods.

> "Return, faithless Israel," declares the LORD, "I will frown on you no longer, for I am faithful," declares the LORD, "I will not be angry forever. Only acknowledge your guilt—you have rebelled against the LORD your God, you have scattered your favors to foreign gods under every spreading tree, and have not obeyed me," declares the LORD. (Jeremiah 3:12–13)

The Lord is always ready to forgive a truly repentant heart, but remember the promise, "God opposes the proud but shows favor to the humble" (James 4:6). When we walk away from God's guidance and become prideful, God will oppose us in an attempt to bring us back to him. There were times when Israel would not listen to God and continued in their sinful idol worship. God stopped protecting and blessing them, and they were overcome by their enemies.

> Again the Israelites did evil in the eyes of the LORD. They served the Baals and the Ashtoreths, and the gods of Aram, the gods of Sidon, the gods of Moab, the gods of the Ammonites and the gods of the Philistines. And because the Israelites forsook the LORD and no longer served him, he became angry with them. He sold them into the hands of the Philistines and the Ammonites, who that year shattered and crushed them. For eighteen years they oppressed all the Israelites on the east side of the Jordan in Gilead, the land of the Amorites. The Ammonites also crossed the Jordan to fight against Judah, Benjamin and Ephraim; Israel was in great distress. Then the Israelites cried out to the LORD, "We have sinned against you, forsaking our God and serving the Baals." (Judges 10:6–10)

Israel stepped outside of God's grace with the sinful behavior of worshipping idols. God warned them to repent because if they continued their sinful ways, he would let their enemies overtake them. God will treat us the same as he did the Israelites if we stop walking with him, going to worship, reading the Word, or praying. But when we sin, remember we are only one decision away from God's forgiveness and the blessings of his promises.

If we truly believe God's promises, how can our faith be weak?

_____

_____

_____

How does understanding Isaiah 55:8–9 help us in believing God's promises? "For my thoughts are not your thoughts, neither are your ways my ways," declares the LORD. "As the heavens are higher than the earth, so are my ways higher than your ways and my thoughts than your thoughts."

_____

_____

_____

The Greatest Promise

The greatest promise from God is salvation through Christ. Throughout the Old Testament are many prophecies of the coming Messiah. We have the promise of forgiveness of sins, receiving the Holy Spirit, and eternal life with the Lord. All these promises are given through Christ, the Lamb of God, who became the perfect sacrifice for our sins.

> Surely he took up our pain
> and bore our suffering,
> yet we considered him punished by God,
> stricken by him, and afflicted.
> But he was pierced for our transgressions,
> he was crushed for our iniquities;
> the punishment that brought us peace was on him,
> and by his wounds we are healed.
> We all, like sheep, have gone astray,
> each of us has turned to our own way;
> and the LORD has laid on him
> the iniquity of us all. (Isaiah 53:4–6)

Isaiah 53 is just one of 353 prophecies of the coming Christ.[26] The story of Christ and the establishment of God's second covenant is the New Testament. There are approximately 250 separate promises[27] from God in the New Testament, and a few of the commonly read promises are discussed below.

> Come to me, all you who are weary and burdened, and I will give you rest. (Matthew 11:28)

As we get closer to the Lord, we trust him more and become more secure in Christ. This gives us more peace and patience from the Spirit, making our life more fulfilling and restful. When the Lord guides us through life in the Spirit, we are rarely overburdened. It is when we are leading God that we overbook our schedule. God will give you time each day to be alone with him to reflect over your day and commune with him. This will bring rest to your soul.

Necessary to obtain true rest for our soul, requires giving control to God. God doesn't share his throne, therefore we must step off the throne giving him control, then the Lord well be active in our lives. This relieves us from the stress of trying to control situations in our life, but instead letting God take control as he leads us through life.

> The thief comes only to steal and kill and destroy; I have come that they may have life, and have it to the full. (John 10:10)

Imagine giving God your anxiety, worry, anger, and unforgiveness as he carries you through the day with his love, peace, and strength, knowing that whatever you have to endure in this life, God will give you the wisdom and strength to overcome. A person living life to the full trusts the Lord and overcomes the world (1 John 5:4), living with the peace that transcends understanding.

> Peace I leave with you; my peace I give you. I do not give to you as the world gives. Do not let your hearts be troubled and do not be afraid. (John 14:27)

Peace is a fruit of the Spirit and continues to grow in us as we walk with the Lord. Philippians 4:6–7 tells us that we can give our anxious moments to God and he promises to give us peace.

> And we know that in all things God works for the good of those who love him, who have been called according to his purpose. (Romans 8:28)

In the previous lesson, we learned that God is molding us to have the mind of Christ. We can be certain that God promises to work all things in our life to mold us. Always love the Lord and give him your best; he will work everything for your good and his glory.

> For I am convinced that neither death nor life, neither angels nor demons, neither the present nor the future, nor any powers, neither height nor depth, nor anything else in all creation, will be able to separate us from the love of God that is in Christ Jesus our Lord. (Romans 8:38–39)

Always know that when we walk with the Lord with a serving heart, God promises to love us and be with us. God's love is perfect. Our souls are always protected by God for eternity, and our physical bodies are protected for his glory.

> Therefore, if anyone is in Christ, the new creation has come: The old has gone, the new is here! (2 Corinthians 5:17)

God changes us from our old worldly sinful nature to the new Christlike nature. New creation, born of God, is a good description of the change from the old to the new, filled with the Spirit of God, with sins forgiven and a divine purpose in life. Every day, God promises us that we will become more of a new creation as he molds us to the mind of Christ.

Let us not become weary in doing good, for at the proper time we will reap a harvest if we do not give up. (Galatians 6:9)

If we trust in the Lord and know he promises to give us the strength to endure each day for the rest of our life, we keep planting eternal seeds, walking with the Lord, and never ever give up.

If any of you lacks wisdom, you should ask God, who gives generously to all without finding fault, and it will be given to you. (James 1:5)

Godly wisdom is worth more than gold (Proverbs 16:16). Pray for wisdom, and God will give you wisdom. Godly wisdom will guide you in your decisions and improve all your relationships, including your relationship with God.

To the one who is victorious, I will give the right to sit with me on my throne, just as I was victorious and sat down with my Father on his throne. (Revelation 3:21)

If we are victorious, Christ gives us the right to sit with him on his throne, God promises to protect us from evil and preserve our souls (Psalm 121:7), and those born of God overcome the world (1 John 5:4). These promises assure us victory in Christ if we continue to trust the Lord and seek to walk in his divine will.

If you declare with your mouth, "Jesus is Lord," and believe in your heart that God raised him from the dead, you will be saved. (Romans 10:9)

If we accept Christ, we have the promise of eternal life with God, and God will be with us all the days of our life. It's promise after promise from the Lord; just believe in your heart, keep walking with the Lord, and never give up. Eternal life is your reward.

He who did not spare his own Son, but gave him up for us all—how will he not also, along with him, graciously give us all things? (Romans 8:32)

Know the price that both the Father and Son paid to redeem you to God. Whether you are walking strong with the Lord or struggling in your walk, know that God is with you and never, never, never give up.

How secure are you with God's promise of eternal life?

_____

_____

_____

Explain how the fulfilled prophecies of the Bible help you believe his promises.

_____

_____

_____

Summary

God is faithful, and his promises will always come true. Pray for God's promises, knowing they will come true when you walk with the Lord and wait patiently for him, knowing you can trust the Lord because he is always faithful. Invite the Lord to guide your life and watch for his blessings through his faithful promises. Charles Stanley says, "The circumstances of your life are extremely important. Never ignore them because they are exactly what God uses to direct your life and to reveal His promise to you … His faithfulness is not limited."[28]

Lesson 12: Our Eternal Home

Introduction

God has created an eternal home as the reward for his family. Attempting to define our heavenly home is difficult because the spiritual world is beyond our understanding. Conceiving of heaven can only be done through the Spirit and with faith in God's perfect love. We will read about our eternal life, knowing that God created us to be with him for all eternity, living in our eternal home that he has prepared for us. We will look at the resurrected body, what heaven is like from Scripture, and what motivates our desire for eternal life. We will see how living for our eternal reward can help us persevere through life's difficulties. For those who have accepted Christ, your eternal life has already started and will continue into the heavenly life.

Our Resurrected Body

God created us in his image, and we are created to live with him in heaven for all eternity. According to God's perfect plan and his perfect love for us, we know this world is not our home, but our permanent home is in heaven with the Father and the Son. We are not complete until we are in the presence of God. In this life we are with God and know him through the Holy Spirit.

> So will it be with the resurrection of the dead. The body that is sown is perishable, it is raised imperishable; it is sown in dishonor, it is raised in glory; it is sown in weakness, it is raised in power; it is sown a natural body, it is raised a spiritual body. (1 Corinthians 15:42–44)

We will have a body that is imperishable, glorified, and powerful; a spiritual body that will never age but will live for eternity. No one can see God and live (Exodus 33:20) because the glory of God is so great the human body cannot endure it. However, I believe that when we are in our eternal home in heaven, we will experience all of God's glory, all of his love, and all the fruit of his Spirit. Heaven is heaven because God the father and Jesus Christ are there, and infinite love will flow all around us and through us.

Describe your new spiritual body with reference to 1 Corinthians 15:42–44.

_____

_____

_____

How can we place priority on our eternal soul instead of our temporary flesh?

_____

_____

_____

Our Heavenly Home

> He will wipe every tear from their eyes. There will be no more death or mourning or crying or pain, for the old order of things has passed away. (Revelation 21:4)

We will live in a perfect body with no death, mourning, crying, or pain because the pain, sickness, and heartache in this life will have passed away.

People relate this life to the heavenly life and wonder if they will get bored in heaven. We should ask ourselves, does God ever get bored? Never! God is perfect and is always fulfilled; he needs nothing. In this life, we are molded to have the mind of Christ, and in heaven, we will be like Christ. Therefore, boredom does not exist for anyone in heaven.

> Now this is eternal life: that they know you, the only true God, and Jesus Christ, whom you have sent. (John 17:3)

Eternal life in heaven is being with the Father and the Son. The absolute ultimate for mankind is to be in the presence of God.

> "What no eye has seen, what no ear has heard, and what no human mind has conceived"— the things God has prepared for those who love him— these are the things God has revealed to us by his Spirit. (1 Corinthians 2:9–10)

I believe "revealed to us by the Spirit" means the spiritual fruit from the Holy Spirit becomes stronger as we get closer to God, and when we are in heaven in the presence of God, the fruit of the Spirit may reach infinity since it comes from God. God's glory provides the light in heaven, and living in our spiritual body, we will be filled with God's glory. This would imply infinite love, peace, and joy, which encompasses infinite satisfaction, contentment, and security, all from the glory of God. No matter what God has us doing in heaven, we will always be in this infinite state of love, joy, and peace.

The city does not need the sun or the moon to shine on it, for the glory of the God gives it light, and the Lamb is its lamp. (Revelation 21:23)

In this life, God brings heaven to us in the form of the Holy Spirit. Whenever we meditate, pray, read the Word, or fellowship with God, we are moving into the kingdom, our heavenly home, where we experience peace, joy, and comfort. God gives us this glimpse of heaven to sustain us through the trials and tribulations of this life and to keep us eternally minded of our heavenly home.

Heaven is in the spiritual world, and it is virtually impossible to explain its beauty and perfection. The apostle John tried to describe what he saw when he was carried away to heaven (Revelation 4). He talks about a holy city, Jerusalem, coming down from heaven, a city that shined like precious jewels with the glory of God, a city with walls and gates and a temple where the Father and the Son reign. There is no night because the glory of God provides the light. John explained his vision in worldly terms, but the beauty and love in heaven and the experience of being in God's presence will be so great it is beyond our understanding. It is not until Christ says, "Well done, my good and faithful servant," and we enter into our heavenly home that we will truly know and see.

Describe living in the presence of the Father and the Son.

_____

_____

_____

Christ said in John 17:3, "Know you, the only true God, and Jesus Christ." Describe what you think Christ meant by the word *know*.

_____

_____

_____

Our Motivation to Go to Heaven

An imperishable spiritual body with an infinite state of joy and peace can be a strong motivator. But there is a stronger motivator that tops any other reason for desiring heaven: to be in the presence of God the Father and Jesus Christ (John 17:3).

Through the Spirit we learn of God's love, and as we walk in his will, our love for God grows stronger and our view of God becomes more spectacular. When we pray, read the Word, meditate, and serve the Lord, God grows larger and his love becomes stronger in our heart. Our desire to be in the presence of the Creator becomes an overpowering desire that can supersede anything in all of life. We will find ourselves meditating and imagining being in the presence of God, and our mind connects with the Spirit, filling us with God's love.

Living for Eternity

Living for our eternal home helps us realize this life is temporary, knowing that whatever we endure in this life will someday be no more than a distant memory as we live in glory with God. As we endure the sufferings of this temporary life, we can be comforted by the promise of eternal life, where there is no more pain or suffering.

> I consider that our present sufferings are not worth comparing with the glory
> that will be revealed in us. (Romans 8:18)

Our lives are temporary, and time keeps moving at what seems to be a faster and faster pace. We strive to live each day to the fullest for the Lord, and at the end of each day, we realize we are one step closer to our permanent heavenly home.

> Why, you do not even know what will happen tomorrow. What is your life?
> You are a mist that appears for a little while and then vanishes. (James 4:14)

We only have a short time in this life to live for Christ. Live for eternity and live in the Spirit because everything you do has eternal consequences. It is God's plan for your life that will bring you home.

> Whatever you do, work at it with all your heart, as working for the Lord, not
> for human masters. (Colossians 3:23)

Living for eternity gives our lives meaning and makes our lives fulfilling. Let your life be guided by the Lord, be his instrument to bring Christ to the world, and live free in Christ as he carries you through life to your eternal reward.

How can living for eternity help us live this life obedient to God's pleasing and perfect will?

_____

_____

_____

How can being eternally minded help us to endure the trials and tribulations of this life?

_____

_____

_____

Our Road to Heaven

Heaven awaits those who surrender their hearts to Jesus Christ as their Savior.

> But the LORD said to Samuel, "Do not consider his appearance or his height, because I have rejected him. For the LORD does not at the things people look at. People look at the outward appearance, but the LORD looks on the heart." (1 Samuel 16:7)

God looks at your heart and looks for a heart that is for God, a heart that desires to follow Christ through the Holy Spirit and overcome temptations. But thanks to the Lord for his grace because we live in the flesh and still sin, though hopefully less as we walk with a repentant heart and let God mold us to be more like Christ.

> Repent, then, and turn to God, so that your sins may be wiped out, that times of refreshing may come from the Lord. (Acts 3:19)

With Christ as our Savior and Lord, and with a repentant heart, we are saved through God's grace.

> If you declare with your mouth, "Jesus is Lord," and believe in your heart that God has raised him from the dead, you will be saved. (Romans 10:9)

From these verses we have the promise of eternal life. Heaven is our home, and no one wants us to be saved more than God. He sacrificed his own son to save us.

> This is good, and pleases God our Savior, who wants all people to be saved and to come to a knowledge of the truth. (1 Timothy 2:3–4)

Do not fear, and do not let your heart be troubled. Christ is preparing a place for you and will come and take you home.

> Do not let your hearts be troubled. You believe in God; believe also in me. My Father's house has many rooms; if that were not so, would I have told you that I am going there to prepare a place for you? And if I go and prepare a place for you, I will come back and take you to be with me that you also may be where I am. You know the way to the place where I am going. (John 14:1–4)

Mark Cahill in his book *One Heartbeat Away* says, "God knows the day you were born and the day you will die, your time on earth is finite and fleeting; it has a definite limit. But your time is infinite when you walk out of here."[29]

Explain why God looks at our heart.

_____

_____

_____

How can our attitude change if we view life as a journey, traveling on a road that takes us home to heaven?

_____

_____

_____

Summary

God created man and woman in his image and to live with him forever. This is our purpose for existing, to walk with God through Christ into our eternal home he has prepared for us. Living this life aware that this world is not our home and eternal life is our destination can change the way we live in this world. It can give us more peace and godly wisdom in making decisions because everything has eternal consequences. We are better able to endure trials and tribulations, knowing the Lord will get us through and everything in this life is temporary. "If only for this life we have hope in Christ, we are of all people most to be pitied" (1 Corinthians 15:19).

Live this life to the fullest by living it for eternity. Live with peace and joy, letting the Lord's infinite love and power lead you through this life with his wisdom. Knowing you have eternal reward waiting, walk in confidence, trusting God's perfect love for you. Life is short when compared to our eternal life, and time stops for no one.

Notes

1   "Science: What Is True?" *The Truth Project*, Lesson 5, Part 2, directed by Focus on the Family, (2006, Colorado Springs, Colorado) DVD

2   Brian Thomas, M.S., *"Evidence of Eternity in Our Hearts,"* accessed September 25, 2015, www.creation revolution.com/evidence-eternity-hearts/

3   Dr. Tim Clinton and Dr. Joshua Straub, *God Attachment* (Brentwood, TN: Howard, 2010), 16.

4   Timothy Jennings, MD, *Could It Be This Simple?* (Chattanooga, Tn:, Lennox Publishing, 2012) 22

5   Dr. Tim Clinton and Dr. Joshua Straub, *God Attachment* (Brentwood, TN: Howard, 2010), 51.

6   Ibid., 53.

7   Timothy R. Jennings, MD, *The God-Shaped Brain* (Downers Grove, IL: InterVarsity Press, 2013),30

8   Ibid., 28

9   Timothy R. Jennings, MD, *Could It Be This Simple?* (Chattanooga, Tn:, Lennox Publishing, 2012) 64

10 R. T. Kendall, *Total Forgiveness* (Lake Mary, FL: Chrisma House, 2001), 34.

11 Charles F. Stanley, *Living in the Power of the Holy Spirit* (Nashville: Thomas Nelson, 2005), 4–5.

12 A. W. Tozer, *The Pursuit of God* (Camp Hill, Pennsylvania: Wing Spread, 1993), 89.

13 Rick Warren, *The Purpose Driven Life* (Grand Rapids, MI: Zondervan, 2002), 63.

14 Bill Hull, *The Complete Book of Discipleship* (Carol Stream, IL: NavPress, 2006), 24.

15 Charles Stanley, *How to Listen to God* (Nashville: Thomas Nelson, 1985), 7.

16 "Why You Can Believe the Bible," *Everystudent.com*, accessed October 5, 2014, www.everystudent.com/features/bible.html.

17 Dr. Hugh Ross, "Fulfilled Prophecy: Evidence for the Reliability of the Bible," *Reasons to Believe*, accessed October 5, 2014,www.reasons.org/articles/articles/fulfilled-prophecy-evidence-for-the-reliability-of-the-bible.

18 Lee Strobel, *The Case for Faith* (Grand Rapids, MI: Zondervan, 2000), 10.

19 Leighton Ford, *The Attentive Life* (Downers Grove, IL: InterVarsity Press, 2008), 25.

20 Dr. Caroline Leaf, *Switch on Your Brain* (Ada, MI: Baker Books, 2013), 56.

21 Ibid., 34.

22 Ibid., 35.

23 Ibid., 130.

24 Timothy R. Jennings, MD, *Could It Be This Simple?* (Chattanooga, Tn: Lennox Publishing, 2012) 24

25 Timothy R. Jennings, MD, *The God-Shaped Brain* (Downers Grove, IL: InterVarsity Press, 2013), 27.

26 "353 Prophecies Fulfilled in Jesus Christ*," According to the Scriptures*, accessed October 5, 2014, www.accordingtothescriptures.org/prophecy/353prophecies.html.

27 "New Testament Promises," Christian Assemblies International, accessed October 5, 2014, www.cai.org/bible-studies/new-testament-promises.

28 Charles F. Stanley, *God Has a Plan for Your Life* (Nashville: Thomas Nelson, 2008), 23.

29 Mark Cahill, *One Heartbeat Away* (Compton, CA: DM Publishing, 2005), 230.

Printed in the United States
By Bookmasters